Measurement in Australia
1938 – 1988

Measurement in Australia
1938 – 1988

A History of Australia's
National Standards Laboratory

J.F.H. Wright

Division of Applied Physics

First Published 1988

© Commonwealth Scientific and Industrial Research Organization
Australia 1988

ISBN 0-643-04895-2

Cover Design: J. Best
Layout: A. Little, H. Wright
Final Editing: A. Little
Typesetting: Frontier Technology Pty Ltd
CSIRO PAS (Sydney)
Printed by Brown Prior Anderson Pty Ltd

Foreword

This history was commissioned as one of several initiatives to commemorate the fiftieth anniversary of the founding of the Division of Applied Physics in 1938. We invited the late Mr J.F.H. (Jack) Wright to write the history because of his close knowledge of the Division and his experience as a technical writer. Originally trained as a chemist he had spent much of his career with CSIRO, firstly as a science journalist and secondly within the Division itself where he had served for ten years as Assistant to a former Chief of Division, Mr F.J. Lehany, AO.

Although he was already some nine years into his retirement, Jack Wright tackled the project with his characteristic enthusiasm and professionalism. He researched many background documents, located much archival material, and tape-recorded discussions with surviving key people who had been associated with the early days of the Division. It was a great shock to all when he died suddenly on 13 May 1988, just as he had completed the manuscript and was preparing to assist with its printing. Under the circumstances this book might well be regarded as a memorial to Jack Wright himself.

We believe that this history will prove to be of much value and interest to all who are concerned with the development of metrology and science in Australia. It is primarily a presentation of factual material but inevitably the author's personal point of view on certain aspects of his subject matter shows through. Such opinions are the author's and we have made no attempt to modify his personal emphases.

J.J. Lowke, Chief, Division of Applied Physics, 1980 – 88
W.R. Blevin, Chief, Division of Applied Physics, 1988 –

25 May 1988

Contents

Introduction 1

Before NSL 7

The War Years 21

The Laboratory and the National Measurement System 29

International Collaboration in Measurement 53

Contributions to International Science 77

The Laboratory, Industry and the Community 89

Accommodation and Facilities 119

The Division of Applied Physics in 1988 131

Introduction

The history of the CSIRO Division of Applied Physics is inevitably complex, not only because of the nature of its work, but also because of the concurrent development of many activities. This must mean that any strictly chronological account of its history would be difficult to comprehend and probably unrewarding to read. In this introduction, the overall chronology is sketched and in subsequent chapters, specific themes are discussed in more detail.

Although the formal decision to establish the National Standards Laboratory, the predecessor of the Division of Applied Physics, did not come until 1938, many events of significance in relation to its history occurred earlier. The first attempts to base measurements on agreed units came quite early in human history but it was not until late in the 19th century that the development of international agreement on units and standards of measurement received the attention necessary for real progress. A significant event was the signing of the Metric Treaty by representatives of seventeen nations in 1875 and that date has been chosen as the starting point for the chronology of the Laboratory.

1875 On 20 May, the Convention du Mètre (Metric Treaty) was signed in Paris by the representatives of seventeen countries. The Bureau International des Poids et Mesures (BIPM, International Bureau of Weights and Measures) and the Comité International des Poids et Mesures (CIPM, International Committee of Weights and Measures) were established and the Treaty provided for the control of the BIPM by periodic Conférences Générale des Poids et Mesures (CGPM, General Conferences of Weights and Measures) attended by representatives of member nations.

1901 The Constitution of the Commonwealth of Australia, which came into force on 1 January 1901, included provision for the Commonwealth Government to make laws relating to weights and measures.

1916 In June 1916, the Commonwealth Government established the Advisory Council of Science and Industry to "prepare the ground for a proposed permanent Institute of Science and Industry". It recommended that arrangements should be made for work related to standards, measurements and testing to be undertaken by the proposed Institute.

1920   The Institute of Science and Industry was established.

1921   In April 1921, the Director of the Institute of Science and Industry recommended to the Government a program of research including research in metrology. He also advocated the formation of an Australian Engineering Standards Association and recommended legislation establishing Commonwealth legal standards of measurement.

1922   The Australian Commonwealth Engineering Standards Association was formed.

1926   The Council for Scientific and Industrial Research (CSIR) was established by the Science and Industry Research Act. Among its powers and functions were the "testing and standardisation of scientific apparatus and instruments" and other activities relating to standards and measurement.

1928   The Committee on the Maintenance of Standards, set up by the Executive Committee of CSIR, presented a report including a recommendation that the Commonwealth Government should pass a Commonwealth Standards or Weights and Measures Act and that CSIR should be made responsible for the maintenance of the Commonwealth Standards.

1929   The Australian Commonwealth Engineering Standards Association and the recently formed Australian Commonwealth Association of Simplified Practice merged to form the Standards Association of Australia, with CSIR as its link with the Commonwealth Government.

1936   In July 1936, the CSIR Executive Committee recommended to the Government that it should set up a committee to inquire into the testing and research needs of secondary industries. The recommendation was accepted and the Secondary Industries Testing and Research Committee was established.

1937   The report of the Secondary Industries Testing and Research Committee was presented in January 1937. It recommended legislation for the adoption of the legal standards of Great Britain as the legal standards for Australia, and the establishment of an Australian Standards Laboratory within CSIR. The recommendation was endorsed by the CSIR Executive Committee and presented to the Government.

1938   On 27 January 1938, the Cabinet approved several proposals for the development of CSIR, including the establishment of the National

Standards Laboratory. In March 1938, the Government authorised CSIR to discuss with the University of Sydney the possibility that a standards laboratory might be built on a site in the grounds of the University, and in June 1938 provided funds for its construction. In September 1938, arrangements were made for the National Standards Laboratory to be built in the grounds of the University. The positions of Officers-in-Charge of the three sections of the laboratory (Metrology, Physics and Electrotechnology) were advertised in September 1938 and Mr N.A. Esserman, Dr G.H. Briggs and Dr D.M. Myers were offered appointment in November 1938.

1939 Early in 1939, P.M. Gilet, A.F.A. Harper and W.K. Clothier were appointed to studentships and joined the three Officers-in-Charge at the National Physical Laboratory at Teddington, UK.

Tenders for the NSL building were let late in 1939.

1940 The first part of the building was completed early in 1940. Shortly after, members of the NSL staff started work in the building.

1945 In April 1945, the three Sections in NSL became Divisions of CSIR, with Esserman, Briggs and Myers as Chiefs.

In November 1945, a Conference on Co-ordination of Testing Services recommended the establishment of a union of testing laboratories.

1946 A meeting called to consider a draft constitution of the proposed union of testing laboratories adopted a slightly amended constitution which established the National Association of Testing Authorities (NATA) and defined its structure.

1947 Australia became a signatory to the Metric Treaty.

1948 The Weights and Measures (National Standards) Act 1948 was passed.

Dr D.M. Myers resigned from the position of Chief of the Division of Electrotechnology and was succeeded by Mr F.J. Lehany.

1949 The Commonwealth Scientific and Industrial Research Organization replaced the Council for Scientific and Industrial Research in May 1949.

1954 Mr N.A. Esserman, Chief of the Division of Metrology, was elected to the International Committee of Weights and Measures in October 1954.

1957 A Committee on the National Standards Laboratory, with Dr F.W.G. White as Chairman, and including among its members Dr A.V. Astin, Director of the US National Bureau of Standards, was set up by the CSIRO Advisory Council to advise on planning for the future of the Laboratory. Reporting in November 1957, it recommended that the Laboratory should be unified under a Director and that urgent consideration should be given to the existing limitations in staff, finance and accommodation.

1958 The Chief of the Division of Physics, Dr G.H. Briggs retired and was succeeded by Dr R.G. Giovanelli.

1960 The Weights and Measures (National Standards) Act 1948 was replaced by the Weights and Measures (National Standards) Act 1960.

1961 Following the retirement of Mr Esserman, the Divisions of Metrology and Electrotechnology were amalgamated to form the Division of Applied Physics, with Mr F.J. Lehany as Chief.

1963 Mr Lehany was elected to the International Committee of Weights and Measures in March 1963.

1972 The CSIRO–Secondary Industry Committee (Chairman, Mr H.P. Weber), appointed in November 1971, reported to the CSIRO Executive late in 1972.

1973 The Review Committee on the National Standards Laboratory (Chairman, Professor R. Street), also appointed in November 1971, presented its report in August 1973.

1974 In July 1974, Dr R.G. Giovanelli relinquished the position of Chief of the Division of Physics to concentrate on his personal research. The Divisions of Physics and Applied Physics were amalgamated to form the National Measurement Laboratory, with Mr F.J. Lehany as Director.

1977 A Working Party on Assistance to Manufacturing Industry (Convener, Dr W.R. Blevin) was set up by the Executive in December 1976. It reported in August 1977.

The Report of the Independent Inquiry into the CSIRO (Chairman of the Committee, Professor A.J. Birch) was also presented in August 1977.

During 1977 and the early part of 1978, the National Measurement Laboratory moved to the new site at Lindfield.

1978 Responsibility for high-level calibrations for the Department of Defence and the armed services was transferred from the Materials

Research Laboratories of the Department of Defence to the National Measurement Laboratory. The Adelaide Materials Research Laboratory became the Adelaide Branch of the National Measurement Laboratory.

The Review Committee on the National Measurement Laboratory (Chairman, Dr J.R. Philip) was appointed in July 1978 and reported in December 1978.

The Laboratory became part of the Institute of Physical Sciences in December 1978.

1979 The new buildings at Lindfield were officially opened by the Governor-General, Sir Zelman Cowen, on 23 February 1979.

The name of the Laboratory was changed to Division of Applied Physics in April 1979, with the name National Measurement Laboratory retained for the main laboratory at Lindfield.

In August 1979, Mr F.J. Lehany retired from the position of Chief of the Division. Dr W.R. Blevin became Acting Chief.

The Melbourne Branch Laboratory of the Division was opened at Monash University in August 1979.

1980 Dr J.J. Lowke took up the position of Chief in May 1980.

1982 Dr W.R. Blevin, Assistant Chief of the Division and Chief Standards Scientist, was elected to the International Committee of Weights and Measures in February 1982.

In September 1982, a Seminar entitled "Australia's Measurement System ... Does It Need Rethinking?" was held at the National Measurement Laboratory.

1983 A Committee with Professor I.G. Ross as Chairman, appointed by the Federal Government in January 1982 to conduct an Inquiry into Commonwealth Laboratories, presented its report in November 1983.

1984 A Review of the Calibration Services of the Division of Applied Physics was undertaken by a Committee (Chairman, Dr N.H. Fletcher) appointed in November 1983. It reported in November 1984.

Following the 1982 Seminar on Australia's Measurement System and the report of the Ross Committee, the Weights and Measures (National Standards) Act 1960 was extensively amended in 1984. The amendments included the changing of the name to National Measurement Act.

1985   The Standards Advisory Committee (Chairman, Professor A.G. Klein) was set up late in 1985 in accordance with a recommendation of the Fletcher Committee.

A report entitled "Future Directions for CSIRO" was presented to the Federal Government in November 1985 by the Australian Science and Technology Council (ASTEC).

1986   As the term of the Chief was due to end in June 1987, the Executive in July 1985 commissioned a Review of the Division of Applied Physics by a Committee with Professor H.J. Goldsmid as Chairman. It presented its report in June 1986.

The Science and Industry Research Legislation Amendment Act 1986 came into operation in December 1986. It provided for major changes in CSIRO following the recommendations in the ASTEC report. The Executive was replaced by a Board of eight part-time Members and a full-time Chief Executive (Dr N.K. Boardman), with The Hon. Neville Wran, QC, as Chairman.

1988   On 1 January 1988, a new arrangement of Institutes within CSIRO came into effect. The Division of Applied Physics became one of the Divisions of the newly formed Institute of Industrial Technologies, the Director of the Institute being Dr C.M. Adam.

On 1 May, Dr W.R. Blevin became Chief of the Division.

Before NSL

When the Commonwealth of Australia was formed by the federation of the States on 1 January 1901, the need for co-ordination of legislation controlling measurements in trade and commerce was recognised. Sub-section (xv) of Section 51 of the Constitution specified that the Parliament of the Commonwealth should have power to make laws relating to weights and measures. Some far-seeing people may have realised that there was a need for nation-wide uniformity in measurements in manufacturing, science and technology as well as in trade and commerce, but it was not until considerably later that this need was recognised in legislation and in the establishment of the facilities necessary for the maintenance of a national system of measurement.

Convincing evidence of the need for such a system was provided by the experience of those responsible for the establishment and operation of the government factory for the production of small arms at Lithgow, New South Wales. In 1909, the American firm Pratt and Whitney was given the contract for the supply of all the equipment, including measuring equipment, for the manufacture of rifles. It was intended that all the components should be interchangeable with those of rifles made in the United Kingdom. Although the first rifles were made in accordance with the specifications supplied from Britain, it was found that the parts were not interchangeable. Extensive inquiries led to the conclusion that the tolerances on dimensions were excessive, and the dimensions specified on the drawings were expressed in terms of two different standards of length. Dimensions above 2 inches were expressed in terms of an inch derived from the Imperial Standard Yard. For dimensions below 2 inches, the unit was the so-called "Enfield Inch", a unit based on a standard maintained by the Royal Small Arms Factory at Enfield. When dimensions all based on the same length unit were specified and the tolerances were adjusted appropriately, interchangeability was achieved.[1]

Some people, realising that a need existed in Australia for an effective system of measurement, called for action by the Federal Government. For example, Mr P. Baracchi, the Government Astronomer for Victoria, in 1913 advocated the establishment of an Australian Bureau of Standards. He contributed an Appendix to an introduction written by Sir James Barrett to a "Handbook to Victoria", published by the Government of Victoria for the use of members of the British Association for the Advancement of Science who were visiting Australia. In his Appendix, Baracchi suggested that "in order to secure uniformity throughout the Commonwealth in measurements of all kinds for both scientific and practical purposes, a national institution should be created, combining, in several respects, the functions of the English Board of Trade and the [English] National Physical Laboratory". "A central Commonwealth Bureau of Standards, such as is here proposed", he wrote, "could undertake to supply each State with secondary standards of all kinds, to verify such standards, and to standardise instruments for the public, as well as to maintain under its care all primary measuring standards of the Commonwealth".

In a Presidential Address to the Electrical Association of New South Wales in June 1914, Dr J.P.V. Madsen, then Assistant Professor of Electrical Engineering in the University of Sydney, referred to the need for providing a scientific basis for measurements in Australia. After referring to national laboratories in the United States, the United Kingdom, Germany and Japan, he said "It is highly necessary that such institutions should be developed in Australia". Although later he was one of the most influential people in the activities leading to the establishment of the National Standards Laboratory (NSL), in 1914 he was cautious, saying "There are many difficulties in the way of establishing a Federal institution, and although we must recognise that such an institution must eventually be established, it would seem advisable for the present for the individual States to pave the way by making suitable provisions for State Laboratories .... I am personally of opinion that the prospects of electrical development in this State are sufficiently assured to warrant the establishment of such an institution, which shall deal not only with electrical matters but with such questions as those of weights and measures and the testing of materials generally".

Advisory Council of Science and Industry

In June 1916, the Commonwealth Government established the Commonwealth Advisory Council of Science and Industry. In the Report of its Executive Committee for the year 1916–17, the Council was described as "a temporary body, designed to prepare the ground for a proposed permanent Institute of Science and Industry". One of the main functions of the Council was "To consider and initiate scientific researches in connection with, or for the promotion of, primary and secondary industries in the Commonwealth".

In a section of the Report headed "Standardization", the Committee stated that it had "collected information both from published documents and by personal interview with experts regarding the organization and work of standardization institutions in other countries" and had "considered the probable requirements of Australia in connexion with this class of work". It was of the opinion that work of this nature was "not only of fundamental

Professor J.P.V. Madsen.

importance to Government Departments and scientific institutions, but would be highly beneficial, firstly, to consumers—in bringing about improvements in quality—and secondly, to producers—in the adoption of standard types and qualities, and of scientific methods of control of temperatures, pressures, measurements of time and space, chemical processes and other technical factors which determine the amount and quality of the output of secondary industries".

The Committee appears to have used the word "standardization" to refer both to the preparation of standard specifications for manufactured articles and to the development of a measurement system based on agreed standards of measurement. It recommended that "arrangements be made for the following standardizing work to be carried out, viz.:—

(a) The standardization of scientific apparatus and instruments.

(b) The testing of electric lamps, apparatus, and machinery.

(c) The testing of instruments of precision used in industry.

(d) The physical testing and standardization of materials used in industry and by the Commonwealth Government".

The Committee continued "Though it is probable that many of the standards which have been developed in Europe and America can be adopted in the Commonwealth, it will be necessary for investigations to be carried out in order to ascertain whether such standards are suited to Australian conditions. It is also important that some organization shall be established to act as an impartial authority in regard to referee work. The Committee consider that the work of standardization should be developed, so far as practicable, in close touch with industrial associations and other interested parties, as is done in the United States of America through the Bureau of Standards and the American Society for Testing Materials".

In 1918, the Advisory Council of Science and Industry published its Pamphlet No 1, "Recent Developments in the Organization of National Industrial Research Institutions", by Gerald Lightfoot. Lightfoot, who was qualified in both engineering and law, was Secretary to the Executive Committee of the Council and later became the first Secretary of the Council for Scientific and Industrial Research (CSIR). Referring to developments in other countries, he pointed out that the examples described "serve to show that throughout the world there is a recognition of the fact that the development of national resources is dependent on scientific methods and research, and they indicate also the path that must be followed if our industries are to be so mobilized and developed that they may be prepared adequately to take their part in the great industrial struggle which will follow the termination of the war".

The Advisory Council recommended that "while existing laboratories should be utilized as far as suitable and available, in order to provide adequate facilities for the research work which is necessary, national laboratories should be established" for investigations in five branches of science and technology. One of these was specified as "Industrial Standards (scientific instruments, electrical apparatus, and materials used in industry)."

Institute of Science and Industry

In 1919, a paper by Lightfoot entitled "Engineering Standardisation" was published as Pamphlet No 2 of the Institute of Science and Industry. The emphasis in this pamphlet was on the desirability of developing agreed standard specifications for manufactured articles and he set out a proposal for the formation of a Commonwealth Engineering Standards Association. There is no doubt that Lightfoot realised that the preparation of standard specifications would be of little value without a sound national measurement system. "There is, moreover," he wrote, "another consideration of fundamental importance which necessitates that the national Government should actively concern itself in the standardisation movement. Scientific research work upon problems connected with standardisation is a necessity. This work is based upon the modern view that quality depends upon definite measurable or determinable properties, and it therefore requires access to standard measuring apparatus and facilities .... It is now generally recognised that scientific research work in connexion with standardisation can be done effectively only by an independent institution under the national Government. Thus in England there is the National Physical Laboratory, in the United States the Bureau of Standards, and in Canada the Dominion Bureau of Standards at Ottawa".

Although a strong case was made for the urgent formal establishment of the Institute of Science and Industry and for the initiation of the proposed research, it was not until 1920 that it was set up under its own Act. In April 1921, the Director of the Institute, Mr George Knibbs (later Sir George), recommended to the Minister a broad program of research related to both primary and secondary industry, which included provision for research in metrology. He urged the formation of an Australian Engineering Standards Association and recommended legislation establishing legal standards of measurement. The Australian Commonwealth Engineering Standards Association, the predecessor of the present Standards Association of Australia, was formed in 1922, with Sir George Knibbs as Chairman, but the Government of the day failed to provide funds for the proposed research in the Institute.

Committee on Maintenance of Standards

The Science and Industry Research Act 1926 replaced the Institute by the Council for Scientific and Industrial Research (CSIR), with Mr G.A. Julius (later Sir George) as Chairman and Dr A.C.D. Rivett (later Sir David) as Deputy Chairman. The powers and functions of the Council were defined rather more broadly than those of the Institute. One of its functions was "testing and standardisation of scientific apparatus and instruments and the carrying out of scientific investigations connected with the standardisation of apparatus, machinery, materials and instruments used in industry".

Soon after the establishment of CSIR, the Executive Committee received a suggestion from Professor J.P.V. Madsen, who was by then Professor of Electrical Engineering in the University of Sydney, that a small committee should be established "to advise as to the requirements of Australia regarding the maintenance of standards and the possible ways of meeting these requirements".[2] The suggestion was adopted and the Executive Committee appointed a Committee with Professor Madsen as Chairman, the other members being Professor T. Laby, of the University of Melbourne, Professor Kerr Grant, of the University of Adelaide and Mr N.A. Esserman, of the Munitions Supply Laboratories of the Department of Defence, Maribyrnong, Victoria. The Committee presented a report in November 1926. After discussing it, the Executive Committee decided that further investigations were necessary. It replaced the ad hoc Committee by a Standing Committee consisting of Professor Madsen as Chairman, Professor Laby, Mr Esserman and Mr Marcus Bell, Superintendent of the Munitions Supply Laboratories. Professor Laby later withdrew from the Committee following rejection by the Executive Committee of CSIR of his contention that a physicist, not an engineer, should be its Chairman. He was replaced by Professor O.U. Vonwiller, of the University of Sydney.

The final report of the Committee on Maintenance of Standards was presented to the Executive Committee late in 1928.[3] It referred to a representative conference convened by CSIR in 1926. While this conference had "advised that the progress of Australia, its efficiency in industry, and the effectiveness of its defence system, would be handicapped if some of the facilities which other countries have in the shape of national physical laboratories, were not made available in Australia in the near future", it advised against the proposal for immediate establishment of such a laboratory. It considered "that in some respects such a Laboratory would be an unnecessary duplication of personnel and equipment already existing in other Australian laboratories," and "that the cost of its establishment would amount to a very large sum". It did recommend that immediate action should be taken in relation to the provision and maintenance of uniform legal standards throughout the Commonwealth.

The Committee recommended that "the Commonwealth Government, under its constitutional powers, should pass a Commonwealth Standards or Weights and Measures Act defining the Commonwealth standards and adopting those standards which are legalized and recognized in Great Britain", and that CSIR should be made responsible for the maintenance of the Commonwealth standards. It proposed that these standards should be maintained by the Munitions Supply Laboratories, the Department of Physics of the University of Melbourne, and the Departments of Physics and Electrical Engineering of the University of Sydney. The estimated costs of the work proposed to be done in these institutions totalled £9,500 for capital expenditure and £2,000, rising to £2,500, for annual maintenance costs, with a possible further £5,000 if it became necessary to subsidise the Department of Defence.

The general scheme outlined in the report was approved by the Institution of Engineers (Australia), the Royal Society of New South Wales, the Australian Commonwealth Engineering Standards Association and the Australian Commonwealth Association of Simplified Practice, which had been recently formed.

The report concluded "It is, therefore, a matter of importance to the industrial and economic welfare of Australia that provision should be made

Sir George Julius

for securing and maintaining accurate standards of measurement on a uniform basis for the whole Commonwealth. The development and maintenance of standards of ever-increasing accuracy in order to keep pace with advancing requirements for increased precision can be carried out only by men of high scientific attainments. In spite of the fact that uniformity and accuracy are the keynotes to efficient standards of measurement, there are no national standards available in Australia. With certain minor exceptions, none of the State Governments have developed or maintained standards of a high order of accuracy. The only way in which the situation can be satisfactorily met is for the Commonwealth Government to set up and maintain national standards, to make available copies of these legalized standards, and to provide the ways and means by which comparisons can be made with the national standards".

In September 1929, the Australian Commonwealth Engineering Standards Association and the Australian Commonwealth Association of Simplified Practice merged to form the Standards Association of Australia, with Julius as its Acting Chairman and CSIR as the link with the Government. Julius was able to persuade the government to provide £8,000 in the 1928–29 year for the Association. After a change of Government in October 1929, he also persuaded the new Prime Minister, the Rt Hon. J.T. Scullin, and the new Minister for Science and Industry, Senator J.J. Daly, to allocate the same sum for the year 1929–30.

Although the importance of work on standards was accepted, the Government in June 1930 advised the CSIR Executive Committee that, owing to the "transcendent seriousness" of the financial situation, no further funds could be provided for the Standards Association. Julius lobbied various Ministers and eventually, £2,000 was provided for the year 1932–33 and this was increased to £4,000 for 1934–35.

In November 1935, the Associated Chambers of Commerce informed the Prime Minister of a resolution carried at a Conference that year urging the enactment of legislation for uniform weights and measures. The Executive Committee of CSIR, supporting the resolution, informed the Prime Minister of the report of the Committee on Maintenance of Standards in 1929, and its recommendation of legislation for the establishment and maintenance of legal standards of measurement. After considering the matter, Cabinet resolved "that the recommendation made by CSIR be approved in principle" and "that the matter be remitted for consideration at the next conference of Commonwealth and State Ministers".

Secondary Industries Testing and Research Committee

In May 1936, the Executive Committee of CSIR was informed by the Secretary of the Prime Minister's Department that the Government was contemplating the initiation of research on engines for both automotive vehicles and aircraft. The Committee was asked to advise on how this might best be undertaken. Julius suggested that CSIR should attempt to assess the whole range of problems of secondary industry on which research might be undertaken and then consider what provisions in CSIR would be needed to deal with them. It was agreed that the approval of the Government should be sought for the appointment of a small committee of highly qualified men to inquire into the research needs of secondary industry and to recommend appropriate action.[4]

By July, Julius had obtained Cabinet agreement for the establishment of a committee, with Julius himself as Chairman and W.R. Hebblewhite, Chief Executive Officer of the Standards Association of Australia, as Secretary. When the committee was being formed, a problem arose from the attitude of the Director-General of Munitions Supply, Mr A.E. Leighton. Although initially agreeing that an investigation was warranted and undertaking to nominate a suitable representative of his Department, he later informed the Executive Committee at a meeting that he had been invited to attend on Friday 3 July that the Department had already done what was necessary and that there was no need for the proposed committee. Julius, who knew that there was to be a Cabinet meeting on the following Tuesday, immediately arranged for the Minister, Senator A.J. McLachlan, to be informed of the establishment of the committee and the names of the members, with the exception of the representative of the Department of Defence. He also persuaded Senator McLachlan that it would be desirable for the Prime Minister, the Rt Hon. J.A. Lyons, to announce the establishment of the committee and the names of those appointed when Cabinet had given its approval. Cabinet duly approved on Tuesday 7 July and the Prime Minister announced the decision on the following day. Eventually, Mr J.T. McCormick, Superintendent of the Munitions Supply Laboratories of the Department of Defence, was appointed to the committee and cooperated in its investigations.[5]

The Committee set up several sub-committees, one being a Standards and Testing Sub-Committee. It presented an extensive report and a set of recommendations to the main Committee in January 1937. The Committee was provided with information relevant to the problems it was considering by Sir David Rivett, who was in the United Kingdom at the time, and had discussions with representatives of the National Physical Laboratory and other institutions. In February 1937, the Committee presented a report which included a series of recommendations relating to the establishment of national standards and testing facilities.

The Committee considered that "because of the many complexities that would arise in any attempt to set up actual standards in Australia as legal standards, and the serious difficulties that would attend the maintenance of co-ordination of these standards with those of Great Britain from time to time", the legal standards of Great Britain should be adopted as the legal standards for the Commonwealth. The Committee therefore recommended legislation for the adoption of the legal standards of Great Britain as the legal standards for the Commonwealth of Australia. It also recommended the establishment "with the least possible delay" of an Australian Standards Laboratory within CSIR and that CSIR "take immediate steps to appoint the necessary senior officers". Other recommendations related to provision for testing scientific and industrial standards and measuring equipment, for research in other fields related to secondary industry, and for the extension of the information service of CSIR.

Sir David Rivett, who returned from the United Kingdom at the end of 1936, strongly supported the idea of establishing a standards laboratory but had reservations about the idea of CSIR embarking on an extensive program of research related to secondary industry problems. At a meeting of the Council in April 1937, he said that, in his view, the prime need was a standards laboratory but that "it was unwise to talk about the Council being able to look after all the research problems of the secondary industries unless very huge sums were available for the establishment and staffing of laboratories".[6]

The Minister, Senator McLachlan, attended a full meeting of the Council in April 1937, when the report of the Secondary Industries Testing and Research Committee was discussed. In an address to the meeting, he said, "The action of the Government in appointing the Secondary Industries Testing and Research Committee marked the most important event in science which had occurred in Australia since the inauguration of the Council. The proposals postulated an extension of the activities of the Council to secondary industries, and if the Council could give these industries anything like the measure of assistance that it had given to primary industry, far more rapid progress during the next decade could be expected".

Government Approval

In November 1937, Mr R.G. Casey (later Lord Casey) became Minister in charge of Development and Scientific and Industrial Research. When the recommendations of the Committee were formally presented to the Minister, Sir David Rivett pointed out to him that it was planned that the proposed National Standards Laboratory should be responsible for the establishment and maintenance of the national standards and for associated research but that testing of industrial standards and measuring equipment in general should be the function of other institutions. The Minister accepted this view and the establishment of the National Standards Laboratory was among several proposals for the development of CSIR approved by the Government on 27 January 1938. In a statement on 19 February 1938, the Minister referred to his hope that CSIR would push on rapidly with the development of secondary industry research and said that "there need be no delay on the score of availability of money".[7]

After considerable discussion as to the most appropriate location for the National Standards Laboratory, Cabinet decided on 3 March 1938 that it should be in Sydney, and that CSIR should discuss with the University of Sydney the possibility of a site within the grounds of the University. In formally announcing the decision, the Prime Minister noted that "the primary function of a National Standards Laboratory is to procure and maintain the National Reference Standards and to provide for the verification of sub-standards". But he pointed out that standards laboratories in all other countries, besides the maintenance of standards and the provision of a calibration service, also covered "a wide range of chemical, physical, metallurgical and engineering investigations in association with the

Left: Dr G.H. Briggs, first Officer-in-Charge of the Physics Section, NSL, 1939-45,
Chief of the Division of Physics, 1945-58.
Right: Dr D.M. Myers, first Officer-in-Charge of the Electrotechnology Section,
NSL, 1939-45, Chief of the Division of Electrotechnology, 1945-48.

determination of the properties, quality and performance of materials and commodities".[8]

Professor Madsen attended a meeting of the CSIR Executive Committee in June 1938 and informed the Council of the progress that had been made towards adoption of the recommendations of the Standards and Testing Sub-Committee for the creation of a National Standards Laboratory consisting of three sections dealing with metrology, physics and electrotechnology. Legislation approved in June 1938 provided £250 000 for "the construction and equipment of laboratories and other buildings", including the National Standards Laboratory. Professor Madsen was appointed as Chairman of a committee to advise CSIR on the planning, construction, equipment and staffing of the National Standards Laboratory. The positions of Officers-in-Charge of the three sections were advertised in September 1938 and they were appointed in November of that year. They were Mr N.A. Esserman, by then Assistant Superintendent of the Munitions Supply Laboratories, Metrology Section, Dr G.H. Briggs, Assistant Professor of Physics in the University of Sydney, Physics Section, and Dr D.M. Myers, Research Fellow in Electrical Engineering in the University of Sydney, Electrotechnology Section. Arrangements were made for them to go almost immediately to the United Kingdom to study the techniques used in the National Physical Laboratory and other institutions.

The First Building

With the approval of the Government, CSIR initiated negotiations with the University of Sydney and in September 1938, the Council was informed that the University was willing to make a site available. Information relevant to the planning of the building provided by officers of the National Physical Laboratory was transmitted by Esserman, Briggs and Myers. On 19 April 1939, the Minister gave his approval for sketch plans to be sent to the Department of Works for the preparation of detailed drawings and the calling of tenders. Tenders were let later in 1939, and the first part of the building was completed early in 1940.

References

1.   Mellor, D.P., *The Role of Science and Industry*, Australian War Memorial, Canberra, 1958, pp. 3, 4.

2.   Minutes of CSIR Executive Committee, 19 October 1926.

3.   Published in J. CSIR, Vol. 2, No 3.

4.   Minutes of CSIR Executive Committee, 27 May 1936.

5.   Currie, G. and Graham, J., G.A. Julius and Research for Secondary Industry, *Records of the Australian Academy of Science*, **2,** 16 (1970).

6.   Currie, G. and Graham, J., Ibid., p. 22.

7.   Currie, G. and Graham, J., CSIR — 1926–1939, *Pub. Admin.*, **33,** 251 (1974).

8.   Press Release *National Standards Reference Laboratory To Be Established In Sydney*, 3 March 1938.

Mr N.A. Esserman, first Officer-in-Charge of the Metrology Section, NSL, 1939-45, Chief of the Division of Metrology, 1945-61, Director of NSL, 1958-61.

The National Standards Laboratory nearing completion, 1940.

Group photo of the early NSL staff (with families) who were sent to work at the National Physical Laboratory in the United Kingdom. Adults (left to right): David Myers, Alan Harper, George Briggs, Mrs. Val Harper, Norman Esserman, Mel Thompson, George Bell, Mrs. Shirley Gilet, Pierre Gilet, Mrs. Edna Briggs, Ron Giovanelli and Mrs. Beverley Myers. Location: G. Briggs' house at Oxshott, England. Photographer: Keith Clothier, circa 1940.

The War Years

Late in 1938, the Executive Committee of CSIR recommended to the Minister that three studentships should be awarded to recent graduates to work for about 18 months at the UK National Physical Laboratory and for 6 months at the US Bureau of Standards and then return to the National Standards Laboratory. The proposal was approved and P.M. Gilet, A.F.A. Harper and W.K. Clothier were appointed. Gilet was to work in the field of metrology, Harper in physics and Clothier in electrotechnology. Soon after their appointment, they joined the officers already at the National Physical Laboratory. Late in 1939, three more studentships were awarded to G.A. Bell, R.G. Giovanelli and A.M. Thompson for work respectively in metrology, physics and electrotechnology and they too went to the National Physical Laboratory.

Soon after the outbreak of World War 2, the Radiophysics Laboratory of CSIR was established. As it was considered necessary to keep its existence and activities secret, it was decided that it should occupy part of the National Standards Laboratory building and members of its staff actually moved into the building before any member of the National Standards Laboratory staff.

The outbreak of the war also quickly led to realisation that the original plans for the development of a national measurement system based on the Laboratory would have to be largely postponed and that the activities of the Laboratory would have to be concentrated on work related to wartime production. Some standards and associated equipment were installed. Much of the equipment was manufactured by British firms on the basis of National Physical Laboratory designs and the Laboratory itself provided some standards. But inevitably, most of the work was directed to solving some of the immediate problems of government establishments and firms undertaking production of wartime requirements.

Gauges and Measuring Equipment

There was an immediate demand for the checking of gauges used in manufacturing and the calibration of instruments and machines used in testing materials and products. The needs of manufacturers in Victoria and South Australia could be largely met by the Munitions Supply Laboratories of the Department of Defence at Maribyrnong, Victoria. The staff and facilities of the Metrology Section of the National Standards Laboratory were expanded as quickly as possible to deal with the needs of factories in the northern States. In order to meet the demand for testing, an Approved Test House scheme was set up. Laboratories approved by the Munitions Supply Laboratories or the National Standards Laboratory and with their testing equipment calibrated by one of these laboratories were authorised to conduct tests for conformity of products with specifications. By the time the war ended, about 150 laboratories had been approved under the scheme.

The Metrology Section reported, in June 1942, that most of its recent work had been undertaken for "one or other of the various Directorates of the Department of Munitions".[1] "The field", it reported, "has covered the examination of gauges and measuring equipment, the manufacture of measuring equipment, the maintenance of a gauge store, the holding of the Reserve Pool of measuring equipment in New South Wales on behalf of the Ministry of Munitions and the calibration of testing machines". A year later, it was reported[2] that "approximately 25 000 gauges have been examined for the Ministry of Munitions and the Service Inspection departments. Measuring equipment has been calibrated for departmental factories and gauge makers, and sample components measured on new projects. Equipment has been set up and adjusted in factories. Gauges have been set for Inspection Services. Assistance has been given to makers of measuring equipment, by advice, testing of early models, and design drawings. Tests have been made on machine tools of local manufacture. Training has been given to personnel from various munition factories".

Gauge Block Manufacture

It was soon found that there was an urgent need for gauge blocks, which were commonly referred to at the time as slip gauges. As it was impossible to obtain additional sets from manufacturers in the United Kingdom or the United States, late in 1940, Madsen, as Chairman of the National Standards Laboratory Committee, and Esserman, who had returned from the United Kingdom earlier in the year, agreed that they should be made in the Laboratory.

Mr C.G. Greenham, a plant pathologist who was seconded from the Division of Plant Industry of CSIR to the Laboratory, led the team that undertook this task. He commented later[3] that "trained staff was not available. In fact, of all the staff actively engaged on making slip gauges, not one had previously seen such a gauge". Greenham developed considerable expertise and, under his direction, gauges were made by hand by a team of young women led by Miss B. Paine, a former district commissioner of the Girl Guide movement. Following the delivery of twenty-five sets ordered for the Department of Munitions, further orders were received and fulfilled.

Top: Miss C. Shimmin and Miss M. Wilson checking gauge blocks. They were among the first group of four laboratory assistants appointed. Photo: 29/10/1941. Bottom: Finishing gauge blocks by hand lapping.

It was known that, although the best English gauge blocks were hand finished, a mechanical method was used for producing gauge blocks in America. Some work was done on the development of a machine for lapping gauges and in 1943, one was imported but was found to be unsatisfactory. Further work eventually led to the local manufacture of machines that produced gauges with a finish at least equal to that of the best English gauges.

Several new types of gauge were developed. Stepped gauges, for use in the checking of gap gauges, were made with the thickness at one end greater than that at the other, usually by 0.0001 in. Tapered gauges, made in pairs, could be moved lengthwise relative to each other, so as to change the thickness of the combination by very small known amounts. Saw-tooth gauges, designed for calibrating instruments used for checking the accuracy of screws, made it possible to reduce the uncertainty of these calibrations by a factor of about fifty.

Assistance to Other Laboratories

The Metrology Section examined laboratory balances and reported on their performance and in many cases, reconditioned balances to improve their accuracy and reliability. It also calibrated volumetric glassware used in chemical analysis and collaborated in the development of Australian production of glassware of this kind. Laboratories with potential for inclusion in the Approved Test House scheme were assisted in setting up equipment and training staff. At the request of the Ministry of Munitions, 200 workshop projectors for use in examining screw threads were made in the Laboratory. Bench micrometers and screw-pitch measuring machines were also manufactured. The Section was also able to assist other laboratories of CSIR in the design and construction of special equipment.

Temperature Measurement

The Physics Section was "concerned chiefly with those branches of Physics included under the terms Heat and Light, and with certain branches of Electricity". It reported that "two main branches of work have been undertaken, one, the calibration, testing, and inspection of pyrometry equipment in munitions factories in New South Wales for the Ministry of Munitions, and the other arising out of problems associated with the manufacture in Australia of optical glass and optical munitions. The Laboratory has collaborated closely on the latter problems with the Optical Munitions Panel, of which the Officer-in-Charge is a member".[4]

Facilities were established for accurate measurement of temperatures in the parts of the range of greatest immediate importance. This involved setting up equipment for realising "fixed points" of the International Temperature Scale, mostly specified as the melting or boiling points of pure substances. Standard platinum-resistance thermometers were made for establishing temperatures between the fixed points and it became possible to calibrate high-quality temperature-measuring instruments.

In collaboration with the Munitions Supply Laboratories, pyrometers and associated equipment used with industrial furnaces were inspected and calibrated, particularly in industrial plants in New South Wales. The ability to measure and control accurately the temperatures of furnaces used for the heat treatment of aluminium alloy components made routine production possible where previously there had been very costly losses due to incorrect heat treatment.

Optical Glass and Optical Instruments

The Physics Section was able to contribute to the solution of many problems involving optics and to supervise the design and manufacture of some optical instruments for the services. One important project was the design of goggles for the protection of the eyes of aircraft spotters from damage caused by looking directly at the sun. Another was an investigation of the lighting of aircraft instruments and the development of a system that allowed pilots to see instrument indications adequately at night without any impairment of their ability to see outside their aircraft.

A serious problem during the war was a shortage of optical glass. Before the war, all optical glass required in Australia was imported. When it became obvious that supplies from overseas were likely to be severely limited, production in Australia was considered. Attempts to obtain adequate information from manufacturers in the United Kingdom and America were unsuccessful. Fortunately, some of the Australian scientists who had worked in the National Physical Laboratory visited the United States National Bureau of Standards before returning to Australia. During World War 1, when the United States had experienced a similar problem, the Bureau had undertaken research and after the war had continued small-scale production of optical glass. One of the returning Australians, Giovanelli, was able there to follow up contacts made some time earlier by representatives of Australian Consolidated Industries and to obtain important information and experience in optical glass production.

Production started in Australia in September 1941 and altogether thirteen types of glass were made, in quantities sufficient to meet practically all the requirements within Australia. The glass produced in each melt was tested at the National Standards Laboratory for freedom from optical defects and the refractive index of each melt was determined.

Electrical Instrumentation

The basic equipment for the measurement of the more important electric quantities was installed in the Electrotechnology Section soon after the return of the staff members who had been at the National Physical Laboratory and later, for a shorter time, at the National Bureau of Standards in the United States. As with the other Sections, there was a considerable demand for the testing and calibration of instruments and of the working standards of service and industrial laboratories. Some special-purpose instruments were also developed and commercial instrument manufacturers were helped with design, testing and calibration.

A substantial part of the work of the Electrotechnology Section at this time was done in collaboration with the Radiophysics Laboratory in connection with the development of components of what was then called radio-location equipment. The Section also undertook developmental work on equipment for the services. A fire-control system for the guns set up along the coast to counter any attack from the sea was developed. Initially, information from visual observations was converted into settings for the guns by an electro-mechanical system. More sophisticated equipment developed later used information from observations made with the radar equipment developed by the Radiophysics Laboratory, together with information on wind speed and direction, temperature and atmospheric pressure to provide bearing and range settings. The Section collaborated with the Navy in checking and adjusting degaussing equipment installed on ships to reduce the possibility of detonating magnetic mines. Measurements made as ships passed over a range in Sydney Harbour were analysed in the Laboratory and settings for the current-carrying coils installed in the ships were calculated so that the magnetic fields associated with the ships could be minimised.

Tropicproofing

When military equipment designed for use in temperate climates was used in tropical areas, many new problems were encountered. These were mainly associated with corrosion of metal parts, the breakdown of electrical insulation and the rapid growth of micro-organisms, especially fungi, in the tropical conditions. When the extent and seriousness of the problems were recognised, a substantial program of investigations was arranged. Responsibility for co-ordination was given to the Scientific Liaison Bureau, which had been set up late in 1942 to ensure that, as far as possible problems that could be solved by scientists were brought to the attention of those best able to deal with them. Many parts of CSIR were involved in the work of developing protective measures or improved designs.

The performance of optical instruments in the tropics was affected directly by condensation of water within them, and by fungal growth, which led

Early air warning station at Dover Heights,
Sydney, Australia. Photo: 25/11/1941

to obstruction of the optical paths and damage to the optical surfaces. The Physics Section contributed to the work on these problems in association with the Scientific Instruments and Optical Panel, which succeeded the Optical Munitions Panel.

The Electrotechnology Section was given responsibility for laboratory investigations relating to the failure of electrical equipment in tropical conditions. Much of this work was done in a small building in the grounds of St Andrew's College, some distance from the Laboratory. In parallel with efforts to improve the reliability of equipment in the tropics, it was necessary, in collaboration with the Physics Section, to develop facilities for testing instruments under controlled conditions of temperature and humidity. Various processes were developed for preventing the entry of moisture into electrical equipment and in some cases, it was shown that the reliability of equipment could be greatly improved by the substitution of newly available materials for those traditionally used.

Sections to Divisions

By the end of the war, each of the three Sections of the Laboratory had a staff with a wide range of skills and in April 1945, they became Divisions of CSIR. The Laboratory was ready to resume the development of the facilities and techniques needed as the basis of the measurement system of the nation.

References

1. *"War" Report (for period ended 30th June, 1945),* Council for Scientific and Industrial Research p. 26.

2. *Second War Report for the year ended 30th June, 1943,* Council for Scientific and Industrial Research p. 25.

3. Greenham, C., *Discovery,* **8,** 16 (1967)

4. *"War" Report,* p. 30.

The Laboratory and the National Measurement System

When the Secondary Industries Testing and Research Committee presented its report in February 1937, it recommended the introduction of legislation for the adoption of Australian standards of measurement, the establishment of a standards laboratory, and the development of a coordinated scheme for calibration, testing and certification of gauges and measuring instruments. The Committee's Standards and Testing Sub-committee pointed out that it would be necessary to provide "primary standards such as those of length, mass, time, electrical units, candlepower, temperature scale and radium".

The Sub-committee expressed the view that "because of the complexities that would arise in any attempt to set up actual standards in Australia as legal standards, and the serious difficulties that would attend the maintenance of co-ordination of these standards with those of Great Britain from time to time, it is considered essential that the legal standards of Great Britain be adopted by Australian legislation as the legal standards for the Commonwealth". It was recognised that it would be necessary to establish, for each physical quantity, a hierarchy of standards through which measurements in industry and trade could be related to the national standards.

The Sub-committee recommended that not only the National Standards Laboratory itself should be controlled by CSIR but that "the national organization for reference standards and for the calibration, certification and testing services be under the entire jurisdiction or supervision of the Council for Scientific and Industrial Research". It recommended that branch testing laboratories should be set up in the main industrial centres of the country but that "in formulating its plans for branch testing facilities, the Council for Scientific and Industrial Research should, in the first instance, take advantage of existing equipment and facilities to such extent as may be found reasonably practicable and desirable".

The main Committee was a little more cautious. It recommended that "the Council for Scientific and Industrial Research be authorized to negotiate with authorities controlling testing laboratories with a view to the incorporation of such laboratories, on a basis of co-operation with the authorities concerned, in a co-ordinated scheme for the organization of gauging, calibration, testing and certification services in those centres of industrial activity immediately in need of such services, and to arrange for such services to be operated: and in the event of the erection and equipment of new buildings being found necessary, to submit specific recommendations thereon to the Government". The steps that led to the establishment of the National Association of Testing Authorities and its subsequent development are described later in this Chapter. So too is the sequence of events leading to Commonwealth legislation relating to standards of measurement, and the establishment and development of the National Standards Commission.

Development of Standards and Techniques

Even during World War 2, some progress was made towards the establishment of reference standards. Some of the equipment ordered from the United Kingdom while the first members of the Laboratory staff were at the National Physical Laboratory was delivered and installed. But effort on the scale necessary to provide an adequate basis for a national measurement system was not possible until 1945. Even then, there were serious problems arising from the loss of experienced staff members at the end of the war, and difficulty in finding suitably qualified people to replace them.

It was possible, however, by mid-1946, for the three Divisions to report some progress in the development of their standards capability. The Division of Metrology, in its Annual Report for the year ending 30 June 1946, recorded that some length standards were expected to be returned after being circulated to other national laboratories for comparison measurements, that improvement in the accuracy of length measurements was expected to result from interferometry studies, and that improved techniques for the calibration of survey tapes were under development. Work on preparations for precise calibration of mass standards and of volumetric glassware was well advanced. Testing of measuring equipment in mechanical engineering establishments, started during the war, was continuing and development of improved portable equipment for calibrating testing machines was in progress.

The Division of Physics reported that, with the release of staff from the pressure of wartime work, an effort had been made "to complete the establishment of the physical standards with which the Division is concerned and to put these standards in such a state that their maintenance will be a straightforward matter" and "to organize the testing facilities so that tests and calibrations can proceed satisfactorily with the minimum of attention from senior staff". In the field of temperature measurement, the Division reported that the International Temperature Scale was maintained "from

0°C to 2,300°C with an accuracy sufficient for present requirements" and that steps were being taken "to improve this accuracy to meet any future requirements and to realize the Scale to its lower limit, i.e., to cover the range 0°C to −190°C". Progress was also reported in improving the capability of the Division to make photometric and spectrophotometric measurements and to measure humidity.

The Division of Electrotechnology reported that its work since June, 1945, had "been devoted almost entirely to the establishment of the facilities required for the maintenance of standards and for measurements". The report mentioned the probability that "all electrical measurements will eventually be made in terms of the metrological standards and of the fundamental electrical standards of resistance and e.m.f.". It continued, "Substantial progress has been made, and is being maintained, in this fundamental work and, in the meantime, the available standards are adequate for most purposes".

Developments in the standards laboratories of other countries and in the National Standards Laboratory itself soon led to a trend away from reliance on arbitrary material standards towards units and standards based on physical constants and atomic properties. There are many advantages associated with this approach. If a unit is based on a material standard, there is always doubt as to whether or not its value stays constant. A material standard may be damaged or even destroyed. There is an obvious advantage in the possibility of the realisation of a defined unit in any suitably equipped laboratory rather than dependence on periodical reference to a standard held in one laboratory. It was also found that the base units, such as those of length and time, could be defined and realised more precisely in terms of physical constants or atomic properties.

In length metrology, after limited use of interferometric methods during the war years, post-war research led to the development of interferometric equipment and techniques for routine measurements and calibrations and for the precise measurement of both line and end standards of length.

With the invention of the laser, greatly improved interferometric techniques became possible and there were developments in laser-based methods of maintaining length standards. In this field too, the Laboratory has been active, and the metre is currently maintained with an uncertainty of about 1 in 10^{10}. Improved techniques and equipment have been developed for the measurement not only of length but also of the many related quantities that are of significance in industry, science and commerce, and for the calibration of measuring instruments.

Although there have been many proposals for the definition of the kilogram in terms of atomic properties, it is still defined, as in 1889, as the mass of

A hydrogen maser built in the Laboratory. This is one of the group of instruments used to maintain Australia's standards of frequency and time interval.

the International Prototype Kilogram, which is held at the International Bureau of Weights and Measures in Paris. No proposal for re-definition so far has offered comparable reproducibility or sufficient advantage over the long-existing definition to lead to international agreement for change. But in the National Standards Laboratory, as in other standards laboratories, there were significant advances in techniques for the measurement of mass and calibration of mass standards. Concurrently, the Laboratory made advances in the measurement of force, pressure, density, volume and other quantities related to mass.

In 1967, the second was re-defined in terms of a property of the caesium-133 atom. The Laboratory's standards of time interval and frequency now include, in addition to commercially supplied caesium clocks, two hydrogen masers developed in the Laboratory.

Calibrations and measurements of electrical quantities over a wide range of frequencies can be undertaken. The electrical units are defined in terms of the units of length, mass and time, but considerable technical difficulties prevented the realisation of the units with adequate precision for many years. So-called "international units" based on the standards maintained in some of the older national laboratories were in use until 1948. With

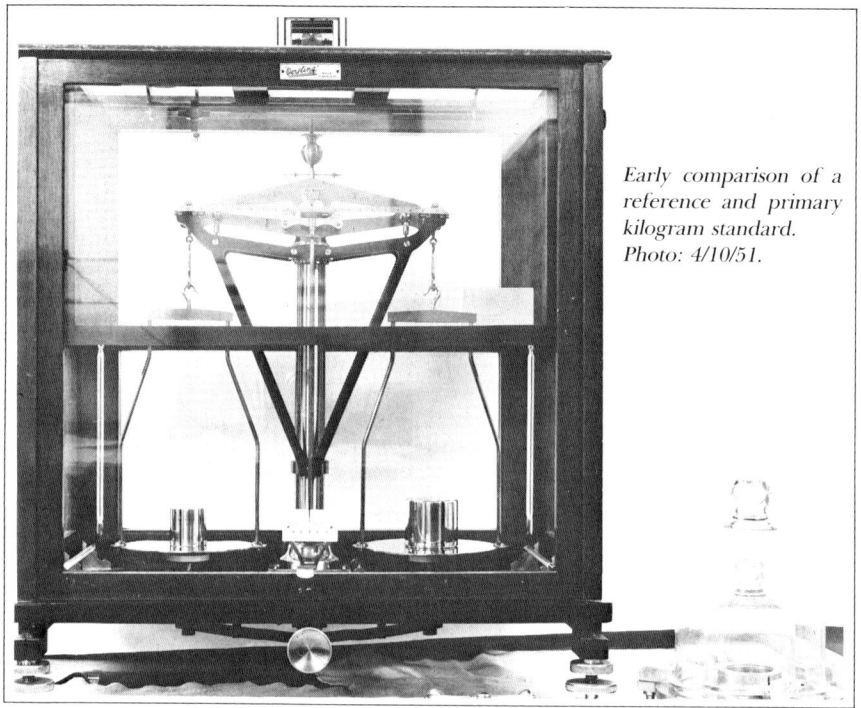

Early comparison of a reference and primary kilogram standard. Photo: 4/10/51.

the rapid development of electronic equipment in the post-war years, there was an increasing demand for more precise measurement of the electrical quantities involved and this led, in the National Standards Laboratory, to a study of techniques for precise measurement of small capacitances. Research work in the Laboratory eventually led to the development of a capacitor whose capacitance could be determined very accurately from a single length measurement. In turn, this provided the basis for an absolute determination of the value of the ohm in terms of the basic physical units.

In temperature measurement, the Laboratory was faced with the necessity of establishing a temperature scale locally. It was able to make use of knowledge of the equipment and techniques used in the older standards laboratories and to supplement this with innovative developmental work. By 1960, publications by members of the staff were appearing in the temperature measurement literature and the laboratory was making significant contributions to the development of improved temperature scales and to increasing the range over which accurate temperature measurements could be made. In photometry and optics, work in the Laboratory made possible precise measurement of a wide range of quantities, and contributions to international advances in these fields.

33

Studies on the measurement of vibration were initiated in 1947 and have continued, and research has been undertaken on vibration isolation and minimisation. In 1972, work on acoustic measurements was started and this has been extended to include measurements at ultrasonic frequencies.

Organisational Changes

In 1948, Dr D.M. Myers resigned from the position of Chief of the Division of Electrotechnology to become Professor of Electrical Engineering in the University of Sydney. He was succeeded as Chief that same year by Mr F.J. Lehany.

In 1957, a Committee on the National Standards Laboratory was set up by the Advisory Council of CSIRO to review the activities of the Laboratory and advise on planning for the future. Its Chairman was Dr F.W.G. White (later Sir Frederick), at that time Deputy Chairman of CSIRO, and among its members was Dr A.V. Astin, Director of the US National Bureau of Standards. The Committee reported that, while it believed that the Laboratory was carrying out its responsibilities at a high level of efficiency, it considered that the existing levels of staffing, equipment and accommodation were no longer adequate. It recommended that staffing and funding should be increased and that the Laboratory should be moved from the grounds of the University of Sydney at Chippendale to a new site "of large extent, with ample provision both for field experiments and for expansion of buildings over a long period, having in mind the future relationship of the Laboratory to industry throughout Australia".

Noting that the Chiefs of two of the Divisions would be retiring in the near future, the Committee recommended that a Director should be appointed, with overall authority for policy and administration. In 1958, Mr N.A. Esserman was appointed as Director, while continuing as Chief of the Division of Metrology. Late in 1958, Dr G.H. Briggs, Chief of the Division of Physics, retired and was succeeded by Dr R.G. Giovanelli. When Mr Esserman retired in July 1961, the Executive of CSIRO decided to amalgamate the Divisions of Metrology and Electrotechnology to form the Division of Applied Physics, with Mr Lehany as Chief.

Change of Emphasis

When the Laboratory was established in 1938, it was planned that it would be a central feature of what the Secondary Industries Testing and Research Committee described as "a plan by which the development of secondary industry in the Commonwealth may be stimulated". The provision of means for ensuring that measurements made in Australia would be internationally acceptable was obviously necessary for the development of

The Committee on the National Standards Laboratory, 1957.

Left to right: Front row: Sir John Madsen, Dr F.W.G. White, Professor M.L. Oliphant, Captain G.I.D. Hutcheson. Back row: Mr J.W. Harrod, Dr A.V. Astin, Mr L. Lewis, Mr W.W. Pettingell, Dr S.H. Bastow, Mr H.A. Wills. Not present, Mr H.B. Somerset.

Australian industry. In the course of building up the staff and facilities required for competence in standards, the Laboratory acquired a range of capabilities in physics and engineering enabling it to assist secondary industry in other fields.

In recent years, there has been considerable discussion on the allocation of resources to the various aspects of the activities of the Laboratory. In 1971, the Advisory Council of CSIRO set up a CSIRO – Secondary Industry Committee "to review present relationships between CSIRO and secondary industry and to report on future developments in this field". It included six representatives of industry, one academic economist, a member of the Executive of CSIRO and two Chiefs of CSIRO divisions. Mr H.P. Weber, Managing Director of Massey Ferguson (Australia), was Chairman. The Committee made a series of recommendations aimed at stimulating more effective contact between CSIRO Divisions and secondary industry, and at developing collaborative programs of research.

At the same time, the Advisory Council suggested that the Executive should appoint a committee with the specific task of reviewing the work of the National Standards Laboratory. The Review Committee on the National Standards Laboratory included three representatives of universities, two industry representatives and three members of the CSIRO Executive. Its

Chairman was Professor R. Street, at that time Chairman of the Department of Physics at Monash University. Its report was presented in August 1973. By this time, the National Standards Commission (NSC) and the National Association of Testing Authorities (NATA), which are discussed below, were functioning in their respective areas.

The Committee recommended that there should be increased effort to transfer routine calibration work to NATA laboratories and that the Laboratory, together with the NSC and NATA, should "review periodically the adequacy of the total service to the community in respect to standardization and standards technology". It pointed out that the transfer of the Laboratory to the new site at Lindfield, which was then being planned, would remove many of the existing limitations, and called on the Laboratory, after the move to the new site, to "take more initiative in approaching industry, and in encouraging industry to consult with it".

The Committee supported the earlier recommendation of the 1957 Committee that the Executive should plan to have the Laboratory unified as a single division with the name National Standards Laboratory, although it noted that one of its members, Dr G. de V. Gipps, had pointed out that "frequently the use of the name National Standards Laboratory can cause confusion between its functions and those of the Standards Association of Australia". The Committee also felt that there was a need for better arrangements for industry in Melbourne and Adelaide to make contact with the Laboratory. It did not recommend the establishment of branch laboratories but suggested that branch offices, staffed by senior officers with broad experience, could provide contact points for industry.

In 1974, Dr Giovanelli informed the Executive of CSIRO that he wished to stand down as Chief of the Division of Physics in order to concentrate on his personal research and the Executive accepted his proposal. The Executive decided that it would be appropriate to put the recommendation for unification into effect, and the two Divisions were amalgamated to form a single unit, the National Measurement Laboratory (NML), with Mr Lehany as Director.

By this time, the Laboratory had achieved world-wide recognition as a major standards laboratory, with measurement capability comparable with that of the best laboratories overseas. Its staff had grown to nearly 400. In most fields, it was capable of establishing and maintaining standards independently of other laboratories. One significant exception was the provision for maintaining standards for measurements associated with ionising radiation. Although there was some research in atomic physics in the Division of Physics in the 1940s, this was later terminated. CSIRO has authorised the Australian Nuclear Science and Technology Organisation and the Australian Radiation Laboratory of the Department of Health to maintain the national standards for the relevant quantities.

Relations between CSIRO and secondary industry involved other Divisions besides NML and in December 1976, the Executive set up a Working Party on Assistance to Manufacturing Industry, with Dr W.R. Blevin, a senior member of the NML staff, as Convener. Reporting in August 1977, the Working Party recommended that there should be more structured arrangements for relating the work of the relevant CSIRO Divisions with industry, including provision for regular meetings of industry and Divisional representatives and for seconding Divisional staff members to industry and *vice versa* when appropriate. Specific recommendations relating to NML included proposals for new areas of research particularly related to the needs of manufacturing industry and for changes to the internal organisation of the Laboratory to allow more flexibility in research planning. It was also suggested that the Laboratory could contribute to the improvement of measurement techniques related to health and medicine. The Working Party noted that the Laboratory was not well known in industry outside New South Wales and recommended that branch laboratories should be established in Melbourne and Adelaide.

A New Environment

In 1977, the Laboratory moved to its present site at Lindfield, and the development of measurement capability has continued to the present time, although at a reduced rate in recent years. The occupation of the new buildings at Lindfield made it possible to set up calibration equipment on a more rational basis. In many cases, the lack of space at the original site had made it necessary for equipment for calibrations to be set up for use, then dismantled and stored until next required. The better environmental control at Lindfield made the establishment of the conditions essential for high-grade calibrations easier. Some calibration activities that could not be undertaken at Chippendale now became possible, for example, the calibration of devices for force measurement by means of a 550 kN dead-load machine.

The installation of existing and new equipment at Lindfield was a major undertaking and there was some inevitable interruption to the routine calibration work. The re-establishment of the Laboratory at the new site also took place during a period of economic restraint. It was recognised that greater interaction with industry was desirable, but the extent to which resources could be made available was limited. "Staff ceilings", limiting the total numbers of positions available to the Laboratory, meant that, in most cases, it was not possible to make new appointments when members of the staff retired or resigned.

Flexibility was further restricted when the Laboratory was required to accept additional calibration responsibilities. Although the Australian standards of measurement were maintained by NML, the Materials Research Laboratories (MRL) of the Department of Defence, which succeeded the Munitions Supply Laboratories, continued until 1978 to provide high-level calibrations required by the defence forces, other research laboratories of the Department of Defence and government munitions factories. In that year, this responsibility was transferred to NML. The original proposal was for the transfer of the staff who had been involved in this work in MRL, but the eventual handover of the responsibility was accompanied by a substantially smaller NML staff increase.

The withdrawal of MRL from standards and related activities again raised the question of NML representation in Melbourne and Adelaide. Most of the MRL standards activities had been based on the headquarters laboratory at Maribyrnong, Victoria, but the branch laboratory in Adelaide had also been involved. As there was a substantial continuing need for calibrations and other services by government establishments and industry in both Melbourne and Adelaide, it was decided that branch laboratories of NML would be operated in both cities. Recommendations relating to the Laboratory were also made in the Report of the Independent Inquiry into the CSIRO in August 1977. The Report was prepared by a Committee commissioned by the Commonwealth Government and chaired by Professor A.J. Birch. Consideration of these recommendations, some of which were controversial, was deferred until they had been considered by a Review Committee on the National Measurement Laboratory, which was set up, in accordance with normal CSIRO practice, to consider the arrangements that might follow the retirement of the Director in 1979. The Chairman of this Committee was Dr J.R. Philip, Associate Member of the CSIRO Executive.

Reporting in December 1978, the Philip Committee pointed out that "several of the Inquiry's recommendations were based on misconceptions of NML's work and the nature of its relations with its customers. The Inquiry did not distinguish between physical standards (standards of measurement) and non-physical standards (standards of safety, pollution and performance)". The Philip Committee recommended what it described as a "shift in emphasis" which, it said, "will require a shift in resource allocation". It recommended "that, in the future, standards research should not command any automatic priority over resources; and that major standards projects should be undertaken only if they satisfy a number of firm criteria". These criteria were:

(a) the project should contain a significant content of new ideas having their origins in the creativity of NML staff;

(b) it should exploit the skills and expertise of NML;

(c) there should be a real international need for a standard of higher precision than that extant.

The Committee recommended "a conscious and deliberate reduction of the present emphasis on the development of primary standards". To underline its view that the research interests of the Laboratory should be broadened, it also recommended that the Laboratory be renamed the Division of Applied Physics. The CSIRO Executive accepted most of the recommendations, but decided that, while the name should be Division of Applied Physics, the Lindfield building complex should continue to be known as the National Measurement Laboratory.

The recommendation by the Birch Committee that the research units of CSIRO should be grouped into Institutes was put into effect in December 1978 and the National Measurement Laboratory became part of the Institute of Physical Sciences. The name was changed to Division of Applied Physics in April 1979.

Following the retirement of Mr Lehany in August 1979, Dr W.R. Blevin was appointed Acting Chief until Dr J.J. Lowke took up the position of Chief in May 1980, with the responsibility for implementing decisions made by the Executive on the basis of the recommendations of the Philip Committee. In June and July 1982, Dr Philip, then Director of the Institute of Physical Sciences, and Professor J.H. Carver, of the Australian National University, reviewed the implementation of the Executive decisions.

The National Measurement System Reviewed

In September 1982, a seminar with the title "Australia's Measurement System .... Does It Need Rethinking?" was held at the National Measurement Laboratory. The seminar was arranged by the Division, the National Association of Testing Authorities, and the National Standards Commission, with the cooperation of the Confederation of Australian Industry, the Department of Defence and the Standards Association of Australia. The papers presented and the following discussion revealed that, while the system was generally functioning satisfactorily, there was a need for more effective co-ordination of the activities of the various bodies involved. Evidence was also presented that budgetary and staff restraints and changes in priorities within CSIRO were causing concern about the ability of the Division to maintain and improve its measurement and calibration capability. A resolution calling on the National Standards

Commission to set up a representative group to "regularly interpret to the Commission the need for change and further development of the Australian measurement system" was carried without dissent. The seminar was told that "CSIRO decisions and the broad government policy of reducing public expenditure generally have led to a major contraction of the resources available for standards programs. The total staff of the Division, including the branch laboratories, is now 360, as compared with 381 in 1973, despite a transfer of 38 positions from the Department of Defence. Of the total laboratory staff slightly less than 50% are now doing standards work, as compared with about 70% in 1973. In the category of research scientists, who provide the vital scientific leadership, the number working on standards has fallen from about 35 to 20, which is only 30% of the total. There has been no research scientist appointed to the Division to do standards work since 1973, with the exception of two transferees from the Materials Research Laboratories. During this period 11 research scientists working on standards, mostly of very senior rank, have retired and several have transferred to other research".

A Committee with Professor I.G. Ross, Deputy Vice-Chancellor of the Australian National University, as Chairman was set up by the Federal Government in January 1982 to conduct an Inquiry into Commonwealth Laboratories. It presented its Report in November 1983. The Division of Applied Physics was one of the laboratories examined. The Committee noted that "recently, and especially after the Division moved to its new building, resources have been moved away from standards work towards applied physics. There have been no new permanent appointments in standards research for a good many years, though we understand that no further contraction in that area is planned. At the same time, the perception of many users of the calibration services is that those services have deteriorated".

The Committee expressed the hope that "the standards function of the Division of Applied Physics will stabilise, at an appropriate level, within the [CSIRO], will be supported by active research in particular areas, and will meet community needs for calibration services in a manner which is satisfactory to both sides". It recommended that "the standards function be restored to greater prominence in the name of the laboratory and the usages adopted by CSIRO", suggesting that the Division of Applied Physics be renamed the National Measurement Standards Laboratory.

It also recommended that further efforts should be made to stimulate development of calibration services within the framework of NATA and suggested that this should be encouraged by increasing the fees charged for calibrations by the Division, with a new basis for fixing appropriate fee levels. Arguing that a more formal arrangement for "dialogue between the

Division of Applied Physics and users of the standards service" was desirable, the Committee recommended that the National Standards Commission be empowered to act as the co-ordinating body.

In November 1983, the Executive of CSIRO commissioned a Review of the Calibration Services of the Division of Applied Physics by a Committee chaired by Dr N.H. Fletcher, Director of the CSIRO Institute of Physical Sciences. The Committee, of course, had available the recommendations of the Ross Committee. Reporting in November 1984, it noted "that the Division enjoys an excellent reputation in the international metrology community because of its many contributions to measurement science, some of which have been highly significant. Within the Australian community, however, there has been increasing dissatisfaction about the promptness and efficiency of calibration services provided in certain areas and about the lack of ability to provide calibrations in other areas that are becoming increasingly important".

The Committee recognised that "although the interface with metrology in other countries is generally satisfactory, and the quality of Australia's standards is well and favourably known to other first-line national standards laboratories, this recognition does not extend to industries overseas". "This problem", it continued, "has surfaced in negotiations for offset manufacture agreements in aircraft and aerospace industries, which are demanding traceability to American (NBS) standards. In one particular case, the Division is participating in a tripartite measurement assurance program with Hughes Aircraft and Philips, aimed at supporting Philips in fulfilling its quality assurance obligations in offset contracts". Noting that bilateral recognition agreements were at the time being negotiated between the national standards laboratories of several other countries, the Committee wrote that "the excellent record of the Division of Applied Physics in the field of standards makes it a very acceptable partner for bilateral recognition, and the Division should be able to conclude such agreement with the standards laboratories of Australia's important trade partners as a matter of course". It formally recommended the negotiation of such agreements. Since then, agreements have been concluded with the national laboratories of the United Kingdom, the United States and Canada, and negotiations are proceeding for similar agreements with the New Zealand Physics and Engineering Laboratory.

Obviously, such agreements depend on the maintenance of measurement capability at a level sufficient to satisfy the other national laboratories involved and any significant decline in capability could result in withdrawal of recognition. The Committee expressed its concern that "staffing may have been reduced to an inadequate level" and recommended a review of staffing when further automation of calibrations had been introduced and

Dr Bill Blevin representing the Australian National Measurement Laboratory and Dr Ernest Ambler representing the US National Bureau of Standards exchange formal documents acknowledging the equivalence of six primary Australian and American physical standards. This mutual recognition of equivalence underpins much of Australia's export of high technology products.

some additional equipment installed. It pointed out "the urgent need to replace key standards scientists by young research scientists, with sufficient overlap in time to allow the transfer of expertise". Some additional funds were provided in the following year for automation of calibrations and for the appointment of new staff in anticipation of some retirements but this funding was not continued in later years.

Following the report of the Fletcher Committee, the division was re-arranged into a Measurement Science Section and a Physics and Technology Section. A further recommendation of the Committee was that "CSIRO should take the initiative in setting up a high level Standards Advisory Committee involving the Division of Applied Physics, the National Standards Commission, the National Association of Testing Authorities, the Defence Calibration Committee and representatives of other Government users (eg. Telecom) and industry as necessary, to advise CSIRO on a continuing basis on the adequacy of calibration services offered and on planning for future standards and calibration needs".

The Standards Advisory Committee was set up in 1985 with Professor

A.G. Klein, of the University of Melbourne, as Chairman. The Committee has met twice a year since November 1985. It has contributed to the making of decisions on priorities for new standards and calibration services in areas such as optical fibre measurements, calibration of digital voltmeters, and calibrations and measurements relating to ultrasonics, acoustics and vibration.

As the term of the Chief was due to end in June 1987, the CSIRO Executive in July 1985 commissioned a further Review of the Division of Applied Physics. The Chairman of the Review Committee was Professor H.J. Goldsmid, of the Department of Applied Physics, University of New South Wales. The emphasis in its terms of reference was on interaction with industry and on research of direct relevance to industry, but it was asked to comment, and if appropriate, recommend on —

(a) the desirability or otherwise of separating the present Division into two co-located Divisions, one concerned with standards, calibration and measurement related research, and one concerned with more general aspects of applied physics,

(b) the name(s) of the Division(s).

The Committee recorded that the Division "represents a huge resource of expertise and facilities from which the nation benefits. The management of this resource and the mechanisms for ensuring that the resource is tapped more effectively by potential users, have been the subject of numerous reviews over the last seven years. The reviews have been useful, and necessary. They have resulted in a major shift of emphasis in the Division's activities to accommodate the new directions to which CSIRO as a whole is committed".

The Committee recommended that "the present activities should remain the responsibilities of a single Division in the Institute of Physical Sciences", and that "the name of the Division should remain the Division of Applied Physics but the name National Measurement Laboratory should be used in communications and documentation relating to standards and calibration activities". It also favoured the Branch Laboratories in Melbourne and Adelaide being known as the National Measurement Laboratory, Melbourne Branch and the National Measurement Laboratory, Adelaide Branch.

The problems of maintaining a satisfactory calibration service that were noted by the Ross and Fletcher Committees seem to have been given little attention by the Goldsmid Committee. It recommended that there should be a further increase in calibration fees, that user support should be sought for the development of calibration facilities where there is a limited demand for such facilities, and that priorities of proposals for new calibration facilities should be assessed realistically against existing calibration commitments.

In its concluding paragraph, the Committee said "It is important that the Division be now allowed to get on with its mission for at least 5 years without further reviews". After eight reviews in fourteen years, that seems to have been a sensible suggestion.

Change at the Top

In May 1985, the Federal Government asked the Australian Science and Technology Council (ASTEC) to examine and report on government-funded research in Australia and in particular, the implications of its findings for the future of CSIRO. A report entitled "Future Directions for CSIRO", was presented in November 1985. It recommended "that CSIRO's main role be the conduct of applications oriented research combined with a commitment to ensuring the effective transfer of its research results to end users". It recommended that the existing Executive should be replaced by a Board, all of its members except the Chief Executive being part-time.

In September 1986, the Science and Industry Legislation Amendment Bill 1986 was introduced in the Federal Parliament. The Bill provided for amendment of the Science and Industry Research Act 1949 and incorporated most of the ASTEC recommendations. The amended Act came into operation on 5 December 1986.

The Board which replaced the former Executive of CSIRO sought the advice of management consultants McKinsey and Co. on the structure and functioning of the Organisation. One of the changes recommended was the introduction of a new system of Institutes. In view of the uncertainty about the place of the Division in the new structure, the appointment of a Chief of the Division, which was due in the middle of 1987, was delayed and Dr Lowke continued as Chief. In January 1988, the research units of CSIRO were re-arranged into six new Institutes and the Division of Applied Physics became part of the Institute of Industrial Technologies, with Dr C.M. Adam as Director. In May 1988, Dr W.R. Blevin was appointed Chief of the Division.

Testing Laboratories

The implementation of the recommendation of the Secondary Industries Testing and Research Committee, in its 1937 report, for the establishment of co-ordinated testing facilities was also delayed by the war. In 1943, discussion of proposals for the development of the testing facilities of the

New South Wales Government Railways led to the holding of a conference to discuss the general question of testing and the relations between the National Standards Laboratory and testing laboratories. The conference, on 26 October 1943, was attended by representatives of the New South Wales Government Railways, the Standards Association of Australia and CSIR. The conference concluded that there was a need for a co-ordinated scheme of "approved laboratories" able to undertake tests and to issue certificates. It suggested that CSIR should be the "central co-ordinating authority", with responsibility for assessing the competence of laboratories that might be approved within the scheme.

The proposals arising from this conference were not taken up immediately but in 1945, a Committee on Standards and Testing headed by Sir John Madsen was set up by the Executive Committee of CSIR to consider a range of matters relating to testing and calibration, including the organisation and co-ordination of testing laboratories, and legislation relating to weights and measures. It included representatives of the Associated Chambers of Manufactures, the Ministry of Post-War Reconstruction, the Ministry of Munitions and the Standards Association of Australia, as well as CSIR. Its discussions led to agreement that the best use would be made of existing facilities through the formation on a voluntary basis of a union or association of testing establishments. At one stage, the name National Union of Testing Services was considered but apparently was rejected because of the unfortunate acronym.

At a meeting in June 1945, the Committee recommended that CSIR should arrange for the Commonwealth Government to invite the State Governments to nominate delegates to a conference to consider the formation of a co-ordinating body. The Conference on Co-ordination of Testing Services was held in Melbourne in November 1945 and was attended by representatives of all the States as well as appropriate Commonwealth Departments, the Standards Association and CSIR. The conference resolved "That this Conference is of the opinion that the desired objective could be attained by formation on a purely voluntary basis of a Union of testing laboratories which desire to collaborate in the work. Such laboratories would retain their present autonomy, and would continue to perform their existing functions, but in addition would be licensed to endorse certificates of test, which would have Commonwealth wide recognition, indicating that such tests had been carried out in accordance with procedure agreed on by members of the Union" . A later resolution replaced "Union" by "Association".

Some of those taking part suggested that the proposed body should be confined to government laboratories but the resolution finally carried was "That this Conference recommends that the affairs of the Association be managed by a Committee composed of representatives of the collaborating laboratories in each State, and of the Standards Association of Australia, the Council for Scientific and Industrial Research, the Associated Chambers of Manufactures, and Munitions Supply Laboratories".

A further meeting on 3 July 1946 was informed that the proposals of the November 1945 conference had been approved by the Federal Cabinet and endorsed by the six State Governments. A draft constitution for the Association, prepared by CSIR, was considered and, after some amendment, adopted. It provided for the establishment of the National Association of Testing Authorities (NATA), consisting, as members, of "those Commonwealth and State Departments, other instrumentalities, organisations, and persons operating testing laboratories which desire their laboratories to act as collaborating laboratories in providing a national testing service and the laboratories of which are accepted by the Association for registration". The Constitution provided for a State Committee in each State and for the affairs of the Association to be controlled by a Council consisting of representatives of the Commonwealth and State Governments, the Associated Chambers of Manufactures, the Standards Association of Australia and one member elected by each of the State Committees.

Following approval of the Constitution by the Commonwealth and State Governments, the first meeting of the Council of the Association was held in February 1947. In December 1948, the Council adopted regulations relating to the procedures of the Association, and in particular, to the requirements and procedure for registration of laboratories. The regulations provided for the formation of Registration Advisory Committees for the various fields of testing, and specified criteria for registration. Before a laboratory could be approved for registration and given the right to issue certificates of test with the authority of the Association, it had to satisfy the Council that it was adequately staffed and equipped, that its procedures and record-keeping were satisfactory, and that measurements made in connection with testing were traceable to the relevant Commonwealth standards.

The National Standards Laboratory thus became involved in two aspects of the functioning of NATA. Calibration of standards and instruments used in testing had to be undertaken either by the National Standards Laboratory itself or by laboratories holding standards calibrated by the Laboratory. When laboratories were assessed, in many cases the people undertaking the assessment were members of the staff of the Laboratory. There have been many changes in details of procedures, but the same principles still apply. Traceability of standards to NML is still a requirement for NATA approval of laboratories and the assessment of laboratories continues to make considerable demands on the time of NML staff members.

Precision calibration underway at the NATA registered Sydney County Council Electrical Standards Laboratory. Photo: Sept. 1971.

Although the initiative for the establishment of NATA came from CSIR, it is now an independent body and there is no longer automatic representation of CSIRO on its Council. It continues to provide an effective link between the National Measurement Laboratory and laboratories serving those in industry and the community who require reliable measurements.

Legislation on Weights and Measures

The Secondary Industries Testing and Research Committee in 1937 also recommended that there should be Commonwealth legislation, as provided in Section 51 of the Constitution, to establish standards of measurement for Australia. The recommendation was "That legislation should be introduced in order to provide for the adoption of the legal standards of measurement in Great Britain as the legal standards for the Commonwealth of Australia". Further attention to the preparation of legislation was also delayed by the war. By the time that discussion on legislation was renewed late in 1945, there had been technical developments in relation to standards that suggested that the kind of legislation proposed by the Secondary Industries Testing

47

and Research Committee might not be the most appropriate. It was already being realised that there were advantages in defining units in terms of physical constants or atomic properties, and in maintaining standards on a similar basis rather than in the form of arbitrary material standards.

There was lengthy discussion on the precise form of the legislation, involving not only CSIR and other Commonwealth Departments and authorities but also the State Governments and the authorities responsible for weights and measures in the States. The Weights and Measures (National Standards) Bill 1948 eventually was introduced in the Federal Parliament in June 1948. In his Second Reading Speech, the Minister in Charge of CSIR, Mr J.J. Dedman, pointed out that, at the Premiers' Conference in 1936, it had been resolved that if the Commonwealth Government enacted legislation covering the establishment of Commonwealth standards of measurement, the States would fully cooperate in the adoption of such standards throughout Australia. He explained that the Bill provided for the establishment of Commonwealth units and standards not only for the quantities commonly involved in trade and commerce, but for physical quantities in general. While the Commonwealth would provide the Commonwealth standards of measurement, the administration of weights and measures would continue to be the responsibility of the State Governments.

The Bill also provided for the establishment of a National Standards Commission of five members "to advise the Minister with respect to weights and measures". The making of regulations "prescribing all matters which are required or permitted to be prescribed or which are necessary or convenient to be prescribed for carrying out or giving effect to [the] Act" was authorised and in particular, provision was made for units to be prescribed by regulation and for these units to be the sole legal units for the quantities concerned. The Bill was passed in July 1948.

The Act required CSIR to establish and maintain specified standards and authorised the National Standards Commission to approve appropriate authorities of the States or Territories as Verifying Authorities which could hold working standards verified by CSIR. It also allowed for improved arrangements for standards for particular quantities to be made in the event of scientific advances making this possible.

After some years of experience under the provisions of this Act, CSIR and the National Standards Commission considered it desirable for the legislation to be changed so as to clarify the respective responsibilities of the Commonwealth and the States and Territories, and some other matters specified in the Act. The 1948 Act was replaced in November 1960 by the Weights and Measures (National Standards) Act 1960. Although it repealed the 1948 Act, it retained most of the substance of that Act. In addition to clarifying the responsibilities of the Commonwealth and the States, it defined more fully and precisely the National Standards Commission and its powers and functions. As the Council for Scientific and Industrial Research (CSIR) had been replaced in 1949 by the Commonwealth Scientific and Industrial Research Organization (CSIRO), all references to the Council were replaced by references to the Organization.

Further changes were found to be desirable and Cabinet approval was given in August 1962 for the preparation of an amending Bill. One of the main reasons was the need for change in the provisions for approval of the designs of instruments for use in measurements in trade. Up to that time, separate approvals were required for each State or Territory, sometimes with the requirements differing from State to State. A Conference of Commonwealth and State Ministers on Weights and Measures in May 1962 decided that the Commonwealth should be asked to set up, through the National Standards Commission, a central authority for approval of patterns of measuring instruments. The amending Bill, passed in May 1964, made the appropriate provision and also established the National Standards Commission as a body corporate, capable of acquiring property and employing the necessary staff. A further amending Act in 1978 provided for some changes in the structure of the Commission and for other changes associated with developments in the technology of weights and measures.

In September 1984, following the September 1982 Seminar on Australia's Measurement System and the November 1983 Report of the Independent Inquiry into Commonwealth Laboratories, the Act was amended again. The amending Act provided for an increase in the membership of the Commission to seven, for the creation of a rational hierarchy of standards, and for the Commission to take responsibility for the completion of the conversion to the metric system. The amendments also included a change of the name to National Measurement Act. The functions of the Commission as defined in Section 18 of the National Measurement Act are —

(a) to furnish advice to the Minister on matters relating to the administration of this Act;

(b) to promote and co-ordinate the use in Australia of a uniform system of units and standards of measurement of physical quantities;

(c) to consult and co-operate with appropriate State and Territory authorities on matters relating to legal metrology and the use of units of measurement in the packaging of articles for sale;

(d) to consult and co-operate with the International Organisation of

Legal Metrology and other appropriate international organisations on matters relating to legal metrology;

(e) to examine and approve patterns of instruments;

(f) to promote the adoption in the States and Territories of uniform legislation relating to —

    (i) patterns of instruments for use in trade; and

    (ii) the use of units of measurement in the packaging of articles for sale;

(g) to provide information relating to units of measurement and standards of measurement; and

(h) to bring about progressively the use of the metric system of measurement of physical quantities.

Since the 1982 Seminar on Australia's Measurement System, the National Standards Commission has organised a series of Specialist Workshops on the National Measurement System. These have dealt with electromagnetic distance measurement, traceability to foreign standards, microwave standards and calibrations, standards of time and frequency, ionizing radiations and flow measurement.

The Australian Measurement System in 1988

Most of the recommendations of the 1982 Seminar "Australia's Measurement System .... Does It Need Rethinking" and of the Ross, Fletcher and Goldsmid Committees have been put into effect. The legal basis of the Australian measurement system is now well established and the National Association of Testing Authorities provides for most of the testing needed in industry and the community. In the Division of Applied Physics, as a result of changes made following the restructuring of CSIRO in 1988, activities related to the maintenance of the national standards and the provision of calibrations are now included within five programs in which they are associated with applied physics research.

The Branch laboratories in Melbourne and Adelaide continue to be concerned largely with standards and calibration activities. The Melbourne Branch moved in November 1987 from accommodation in Monash University to the David Rivett Laboratory at Clayton. It provides a calibration service in engineering, physical and electrical metrology, much of the demand arising from Defence Department laboratories. Recently, the development of an automated system for calibration of gauge blocks has been completed, allowing the Branch to satisfy a large part of the Australian demand for gauge block calibration. Systems for calibration of hardness blocks, surface roughness standards and high-value electrical resistance standards have also been automated and work is proceeding on the automation of equipment for other types of calibrations. Some collaborative research is also being undertaken within the Applied Physics Industrial Program.

The Adelaide Branch, located at Woodville, also provides a calibration service, particularly in relation to electrical and temperature measurement. It undertakes high-precision measurements on the thermal conductivity of insulating materials for clients not only in Australia but also in New Zealand and South-East Asia. The measurements are made by the guarded hot-plate method over a temperature range from -180 to $800°C$. Work is proceeding on the development of a hot-wire method for measurements on materials of higher thermal conductivity.

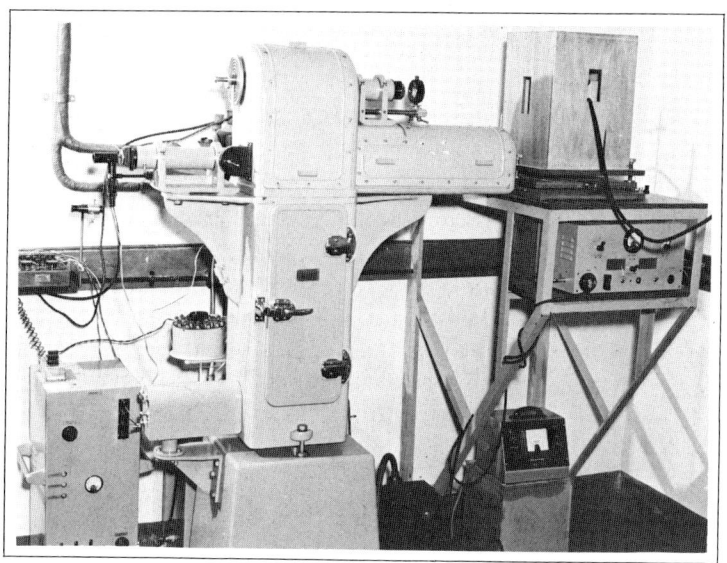

Early interferometer based on Koster's design used for the maintenance of end-standards of length. Photo: 11/3/1953.

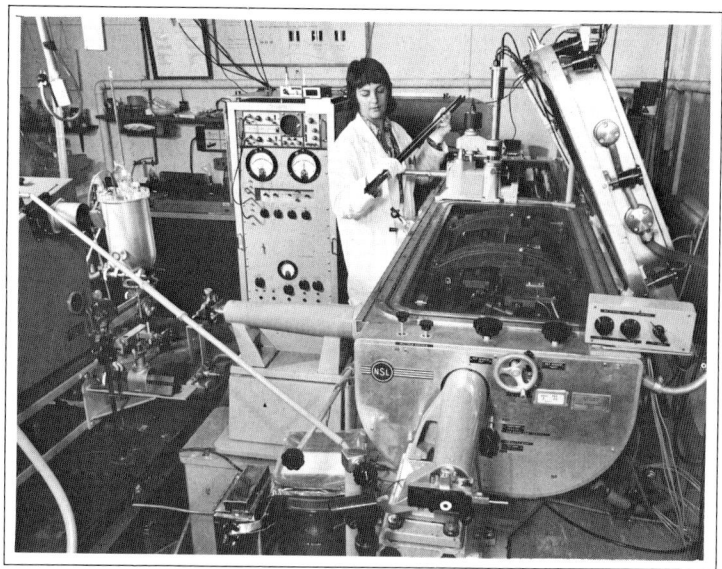

The 1 m line standard interferometer. The wavelength of the krypton-86 line used in this instrument defined the metre between 1960 and 1983. Prior to 1960 copies of the prototype metre – a Pt-Ir x cross-sectioned bar with line engravings 1 m apart – defined the standard of length. Photo: 29/10/1973.

International Collaboration in Measurement

Following the arrangement for the first members of the staff of the Laboratory to work at the National Physical Laboratory in the United Kingdom, there has been a continuing close relationship between the two laboratories. Both have taken part in intercomparisons of standards, some being bi-lateral and others involving a larger number of Laboratories. There has also been continuing collaboration with the National Bureau of Standards of the United States, and with the standards laboratories of several other countries, involving many instances of extended visits.

The desirability of international cooperation in measurement was recognised many years ago but it is only in relatively recent times that substantial progress has been made. In discussions in Europe through the middle years of the 19th century, various proposals for internationally recognised systems of measurement were considered. It became clear that the most promising basis for international agreement was the metric system. After prolonged discussions involving some thirty countries, the Metric Treaty was signed in 1875 by representatives of seventeen nations. This committed the signatory nations to the establishment of an International Bureau of Weights and Measures (BIPM) as the repository of the international standards for the metre and the kilogram. The treaty also set up arrangements for the development of future agreements on units and standards for other physical quantities. The International Committee of Weights and Measures (CIPM) was also established to control the Bureau and to make recommendations to periodic General Conferences of Weights and Measures (CGPM) attended by representatives of the member nations.

In 1947, Australia became a signatory to the Metric Treaty and at the Tenth General Conference of Weights and Measures in October 1954, Mr N.A. Esserman, Chief of the Division of Metrology, was elected as a member of the International Committee of Weights and Measures. The Laboratory has continued to be involved in the work of the Committee and its several specialist Consultative Committees and to collaborate actively with the International Bureau of Weights and Measures. Following the retirement of Mr Esserman from the CIPM in 1962, Mr F.J. Lehany, Chief of the Division of Applied Physics, was elected as a member of the Committee in March 1963. Mr Lehany retired in 1979 and Dr W.R. Blevin, Assistant

Chief of the Division of Applied Physics and Chief Standards Scientist, was elected to the Committee in February 1982.

Although some members of the staff of the Laboratory attended earlier meetings of Consultative Committees by invitation, the Laboratory first participated formally in the work of the Committees in 1962, when representatives were nominated to the Committees concerned with the definition of the metre, electrical measurements, thermometry and photometry. Dr D.B. Prowse was a foundation member of the recently formed Consultative Committee on Mass and Related Quantities. The Laboratory has made substantial contributions to the work of all of these Committees. Some of the relevant research activities are described below.

Re-definition of the Metre

Following limited use of interferometric methods for length measurement during the war, research in length interferometry was continued by a group led by Dr C.F. Bruce. An interferometer based on the design of Kosters was constructed for the measurement of end standards up to 500 mm long by direct comparison with light wavelengths.[1] The interferometer, eventually completed in 1956, was the basis of the maintenance of length standards in Australia for several years. Results of measurements in the Laboratory formed part of the information used in the development of a new definition of the metre in terms of the wavelength of a particular radiation from the isotope krypton-86, adopted by the General Conference of Weights and Measures in 1960. In particular, the first satisfactory calculation of an important correction applicable to the measurement of wavelengths was presented.[2] The design and construction of a 1 m line standard interferometer to realise the new definition of the metre was a major undertaking from 1957 to 1964. The implementation of the wavelength standard relied on additional corrections for geometrical factors, which were first properly evaluated as a result of work in the Laboratory.[3]

The invention of the laser provided highly monochromatic light sources and led to greatly improved interferometric techniques. Stabilised lasers were developed in the Laboratory for length interferometry and are currently used to maintain the metre with an uncertainty of about 1 in 10^{10}. The Laboratory has continued to contribute to the work of the Consultative Committee on the Definition of the Metre (CCDM). In October 1983, the General Conference of Weights and Measures adopted a new definition of the metre based on an agreed value for the speed of light. Much of the information on which this definition is based was derived from research in overseas laboratories involving equipment that was not available in

Optical workbench incorporating stabilized lasers. These are currently used to maintain the metre with an uncertainty of about 1 in 10^{10}. Photo: 4/6/1985.

Australia, but work in the Laboratory allowed members of its staff to make significant contributions to the discussion in the CCDM that led to the new definition.

The Calculable Capacitor and the Absolute Determination of the Ohm

Soon after the war, Mr A.M. Thompson and Mr W.K. Clothier worked on the design of very stable shielded three-terminal capacitors with precisely defined values in the picofarad range and developed measurement techniques using transformer-ratio-arm bridges. They were able to compare capacitances of the order of 1 pF with an uncertainty of less than 1 in 10^6.

At the time, impedance standards were maintained on the basis of inductors, which were essentially coils of wire of carefully designed geometry whose inductances could be calculated from their dimensions. With standards of this kind, only limited accuracy and reproducibility could be achieved. In theory, it was also possible to base impedance standards on capacitors whose capacitances might be calculable from their geometry and dimensions. This possibility had not been given much attention as the values of capacitors of suitable dimensions are quite small. When it was shown that very small capacitances could be measured accurately, the possibility of constructing a capacitor whose capacitance could be calculated was considered, as this might provide a means of relating the electrical impedance units to the mechanical units with greatly improved precision.

Work on the design of a capacitor of this kind was initiated in the Laboratory early in 1954 by Clothier. He proposed to construct a guarded parallel-plate capacitance standard with variable spacing. The parallel plates were to be in the form of metallised glass or fused silica optical flats, and the spacing between them was to be measured by Fabry-Perot interferometry. Errors due to surface imperfections, contact potential differences and differences between the locations of the "optical" and "electrical" surfaces would be cancelled by measuring at more than one spacing. The guarded electrode was to be a square defined by metal-free lines left as the shadows of fine stretched wires placed close to the surface of one of the optical flats during the metal evaporation process.

This calculable capacitor would have had a value of only a few picofarads so that, to make use of it to evaluate capacitances of larger values, a series of very stable capacitors of intermediate values would be needed. Among possibilities investigated by Thompson were cylindrical systems in which the capacitance per unit length depends only on the shape of the cross section. It was thought that, with a square cross section with the faces insulated from each other, the stability of the cross section could be checked simply by measuring the capacitances of each pair of opposite faces.

Dr D.G. Lampard calculated the capacitance of a system of this kind and confirmed that the mean capacitance would be independent of small departures from symmetry. His calculations for other shapes gave the same capacitance per unit length and a very simple and general relation between the two capacitances per unit length of a four-electrode cylindrical system was derived.[4] Experiments were undertaken with a cross-capacitor made up of four round steel bars and good agreement was obtained between the calculated capacitance and the capacitance as measured in relation to the existing standards. These results confirmed the possibility of a calculable standard whose capacitance could be calculated from a single length measurement.

It was agreed with Clothier that he would set aside his own proposal and design and construct a cross-capacitor, with provision for changing the effective length by means of a movable tube between four outer bars. This

Mr H. Bairnsfather and Mr M.C. McGregor conducting measurements using the Laboratory's calculable capacitor. The four cylindrical electrodes (not visible) are housed within the evacuated cylindrical casing (centre). Photo: 19/12/1962.

would make it possible, by measuring differences between the capacitances at two or more settings of the inner tube, to avoid the difficult task of measuring the effective length accurately. The distances through which the guard tube was moved could be measured by optical interferometry, with the optical path through the tube, and the change in capacitance could be calculated from the change in effective length. A long series of experiments conducted in collaboration with Mr M.C. McGregor and Mr H. Bairnsfather provided the design parameters and led to many refinements.

The instrument in its final form[5] made available calculated capacitances up to approximately 0.25 pF, with an uncertainty estimated to be about 1 in 10^7. Conversion from electrostatic units to units in the International System involves the speed of light. Initially, this introduced another uncertainty of about 1 in 10^6, but the redefinition of the metre in 1983 made the speed of light a defined constant and so removed this uncertainty completely.

The availability of accurately known capacitances made it possible to undertake an absolute determination of the value of the ohm. The ohm had been maintained by reference to calculable inductors, with an uncertainty of a few parts in 10^6. In the technique developed by Thompson and his co-workers[6], ac bridge methods were used to compare fixed capacitors calibrated against the calculable capacitor, through a build-up process, with capacitors of larger values and finally with a 10 000 Ω resistor in a frequency-dependent bridge.

As the accuracy of the calculated capacitances was greatest at values of about ⅙ pF, the build-up process was based on capacitors of this value. Three ⅙ pF capacitors, each calibrated against the calculable capacitor, were connected in parallel to give a value close to 0.5 pF. This was used as the basis for the build-up, with a 10:1 transformer-ratio-arm bridge, to 5 pF, 50 pF, 500 pF, and 5000 pF, the value needed for the bridge in which the 10 000 Ω resistor was evaluated in terms of capacitance and frequency.

It was then necessary to compare this 10 000 Ω resistor with a 1 Ω standard resistor. This was done initially in two steps using a built-up resistor developed in the Laboratory by Mr B.V. Hamon.[7] The resistor consisted essentially of ten matched resistors, which could be connected either in series through special junctions or in parallel by means of a weighting network of additional resistors. With values of the individual resistors differing by less than 1 in 10^4, the ratio of the series resistance to the parallel resistance was 100, with an uncertainty of about 1 in 10^8. In the final comparison a 100 Ω build-up resistor was constructed to give the desired 1 to 10 000 ratio directly. Hamon's build-up principle has been widely used in metrology laboratories around the world.

Considerable interest in the work in the Laboratory on capacitance measurement and the development of the calculable capacitor was taken by scientists from the US National Bureau of Standards. Thompson visited the Bureau late in 1956, and in 1957 Dr F.K. Harris, who was in charge of work on electrical measurements in the Bureau, visited NSL. Later in that year, Dr A.V. Astin, Director of the Bureau of Standards, also visited the Laboratory to assist the work of a Review Committee set up to advise on its future activities. In September 1957, McGregor went to the Bureau of Standards for six months to work in collaboration with scientists there on a calculable capacitor of similar design to the one at NSL. Further collaborative work led to an arrangement for Mr R.D. Cutkosky, a member of the staff of the Bureau, to work at NSL for three months in 1960 with the group concerned with the calculable capacitor and the absolute determination of the ohm.

In 1965, Lampard and Thompson were jointly awarded the Albert F. Sperry Medal of the Instrument Society of America for their contributions to the improvement of fundamental international standards of capacitance

 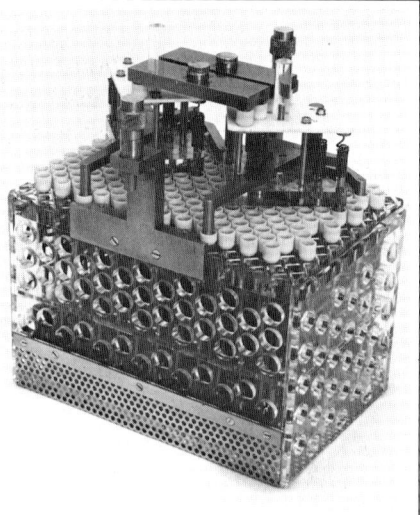

The 100 × 100 Ω build up resistor.

Left: An early stage of construction showing the very low temperature coefficient wire wound resistors connected to electrolytic copper terminals embedded in a Perspex block which provides high electrical insulation. The first row shows the slots on the outer pair of potential terminals. These slots form part of the 4 terminal junction and can be adjusted to ensure the current leads from the connecting resistors are centrally tapped. The four unslotted central rods are current terminals.

Right: The finished resistor. Teflon caps on the resistor terminals contain mercury. This amalgamates with the copper surface to provide low resistance electrical contact. The two centre bars form the voltage terminals of the final resistor while the current terminals are on the edge of the Perspex lid. In operation the resistor is immersed in a temperature controlled oil bath and the holes in the container allow circulation of the oil.

and resistance. This was only the seventh award of the medal and the first to Australian research workers.

An interesting comment on the work of the Laboratory was made in a talk given by Mr Walter Williams, US Under-Secretary of Commerce, in December 1957. Speaking in Boston soon after the launching of the Soviet Sputnik, he said "There are those who have been disturbed by the recent Russian successes in the satellite field. Certainly no thoughtful person would pooh-pooh these accomplishments. By no means. Yet, it stands to reason, doesn't it, that a nation which concentrates its efforts and resources in a specific field is most likely to be first in that field. Only recently I was advised that Australia—little Australia with only 7 or 8 million population—leads all other nations of the world in one specific branch of scientific research. This relates to precise and absolute measure of electrical capacitance".[8] Of course, Australia had not concentrated all of its resources in this one field, but in it the Laboratory had certainly achieved world leadership.

Subsequently, all the major national standards laboratories have adopted the calculable cross-capacitor principle in the design of standards for measurements of capacitance, inductance and resistance. Since January 1969, the value of the ohm has been based by international agreement on determinations made with calculable capacitors, the main contributing laboratory being NSL (NML). The International Bureau of Weights and Measures since 1964 has used comparisons with the NSL-NML calculable capacitor to monitor a continuous drift of about 5 parts in 10^8 per year in the resistances of its wire-wound 1 Ω standards. Recently, the performance of the NML standard through twenty years of use has been reviewed and the uncertainty in the NML determination of the ohm has been reassessed.[8] The uncertainty (at the 1-σ level) is now estimated to be 6.2 × 10⁻⁸.

Absolute Determination of the Volt

In 1964, Clothier started work on an absolute determination of the volt in terms of the units of length, mass and time. The volt was then maintained in standards laboratories by means of standard cells and regular intercomparisons were made between the cells of the major national laboratories and those of the International Bureau of Weights and Measures. Clothier proposed a new electrostatic method for the absolute determination of the volt using a liquid electrometer. The proposal in principle was to mount a flat circular conductor horizontally above the surface of a pool of mercury of substantially larger diameter and to determine the height of the "plateau" produced by the application of a potential difference of some kilovolts between the two surfaces. The height of the flat conductor above the outer surface of the mercury pool and the height above the top of the plateau were to be measured. The upper conductor was to be a fused silica optical flat with its lower surface coated with semi-transparent conducting metal films and the height measurements were to be made by optical interferometry.

Clothier showed that, when certain dimensional conditions were fulfilled, the absolute value of the applied potential difference could be calculated from the two height measurements, the density of the mercury, and several known constants, only small residual errors due to contact potential differences and other surface effects remaining. He showed that these residual errors could be eliminated by taking one or more additional

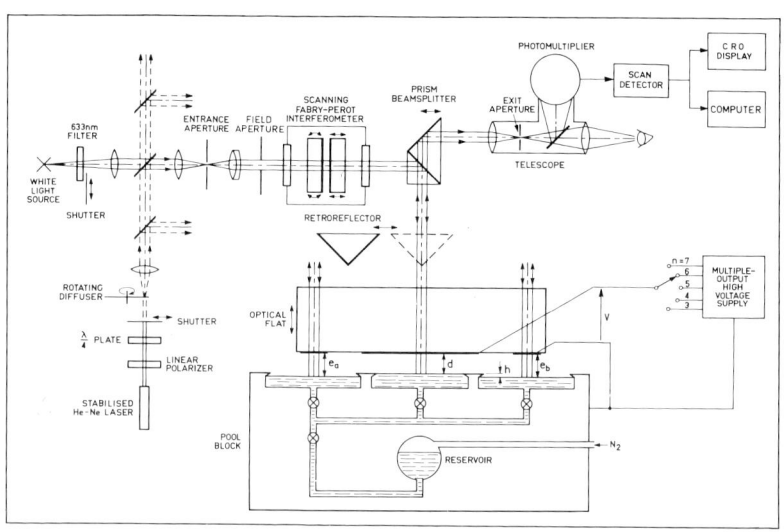

Top: Schematic of the absolute volt experiment. The change in voltage applied to the electrode surface on the optical flat during two experimental runs is given by

$$V_2 - V_1 = k(d_2 - d_1)\sqrt{h}$$

where d is the distance between the central pool surface and the fixed electrode, h is the height difference between the centre and outer pools and k is a constant related to the density of mercury.

Bottom: Final experimental set-up used in NML's absolute volt determination. The liquid electrometer can be seen within the evacuated enclosure (centre).

measurements with the same plateau height but with increased potential difference and correspondingly increased height of the flat above the plateau.[10]

The realisation of this concept was a formidable undertaking, in which Clothier was joined by Dr G.J. Sloggett. To achieve the desired overall accuracy, it was necessary to reduce the uncertainty in the height measurements to less than 1 nm. The most serious difficulty arose from vibration, mostly of seismic origin, which caused the development of waves on the mercury surface. The need to minimise the effects of vibration, among other things, led to a decision to use a set of three connected pools, side by side in a stainless steel block, with the potential difference applied only to the central pool. The effects of vertical vibration were minimised by providing for the upper part of the walls of the mercury pools to slope inwards at the angle to the vertical for which there was no meniscus.

Vibration in the horizontal plane was reduced to an acceptable level by mounting the instrument on a heavy cast iron table supported by three long thin vertical rods in compression. This made it possible to arrange for the horizontal resonance frequency of oscillation of the assembly to be substantially lower than the lowest pool resonance frequency. Silicone oil dampers were used to limit transmission of vibration, and residual wave motion within the mercury pools was attenuated by perforated stainless steel plates dividing the pools horizontally into approximately equal upper and lower parts. As a further precaution against vibration, the distribution of mass was arranged so that the centre of gravity of the entire supported system was at the level of the pool system.

The pools, the upper optical flat and the associated control mechanisms were enclosed in a vacuum chamber resting on three remotely controlled hydraulic supports, by means of which the optical flat could be made parallel with the mercury surfaces. The measurements of the distances between the optical flat and the surfaces of the mercury pools were made by Fabry-Perot reflection interferometry and "optical multiplication" using "white-light fringes". The interferometer system was calibrated by reference to light of a selected frequency from a stabilised helium-neon laser. The light used to form the white-light fringes came from quartz-halogen lamps and passed through narrow-band filters with their pass-bands centred on the frequency of the light from the laser.

It was necessary to compare the large voltages applied in the electrometer accurately with the volt as maintained in the Laboratory and this was done by means of specially designed equipment including a stabilised dc power supply and an air-cooled resistive voltage divider with self-contained means for calibration.

The calculation of the force produced by the applied voltage required accurate knowledge of the density of the mercury used and of the gravitational acceleration at the site. This information was available from measurements made in the Laboratory.

For the final series of measurements in 1983, a computer was used to control the complex series of operations extending through several hours, and to record and process the readings for each determination. On the basis of twenty-seven determinations, a value for the volt was published in 1984.[11] After a detailed examination of possible sources of error, the uncertainty of the determination, at the $1 - \sigma$ level, was estimated as about 3 in 10^7. The value of the volt as determined in this way was greater than the volt as maintained internationally by 8.1 parts in 10^6. This confirmed evidence from other sources that there was a discrepancy of this order. It is anticipated that an adjustment of about this magnitude will be made to the international volt, probably with effect from 1990.

Applications of the ac Josephson Effect

In 1969, investigations on possible applications of the ac Josephson effect in electrical metrology were started by Mr I.K. Harvey and co-workers. The Josephson effects are phenomena that occur at very low temperatures in superconducting systems.[12] The ac Josephson effect was relevant to the development of a new type of precision voltage standard in which voltage could be related to frequency. If a Josephson junction is irradiated with microwave energy, the voltage-current characteristic shows a pronounced step structure. The emf of the constant-potential steps is proportional to the frequency of the microwave source, the voltage being related to frequency by the equation

$$2V = (h / 2e)nf$$

In the equation

V is the emf across the junction,
h is Planck's constant,
e is the electron charge,
n is an integer,
f is the frequency of the radiation incident on the junction.

Since frequency can be measured with extremely high accuracy, this relationship is ideal for the development of a standard.

Harvey and his group constructed equipment for maintaining a standard of emf in this way, using a niobium-point junction and utilising room-temperature measurement techniques.[13] The standard became operational in 1970 and, with later refinements, has been in regular use since that time, achieving a measurement capability with an uncertainty of less than 1 in 10^7. International voltage transfers between the few national laboratories that had developed Josephson-effect standards at that time showed agreement within a few parts in 10^7 between independent and widely different experimental realisations of the standard. Following these successful intercomparisons, the International Bureau of Weights and Measures in 1973 proposed that Josephson-effect systems be adopted as the preferred means of maintaining emf standards and a value for the frequency-voltage constant was adopted. Absolute determinations of the volt at NML and other laboratories are expected to provide a revised value for this constant.

After the introduction to superconducting phenomena in the development of the Josephson-effect voltage standard, Harvey investigated other possible applications of superconductivity in precise electrical measurements. He developed SQUIDS[14] in a variety of topologies together with other superconducting devices specifically related to precise electrical measurements. A superconducting current comparator embodying a new concept that was developed during this work achieved a performance about a thousand times better than comparable room-temperature comparators. The superconducting current comparator has ratio windings within a superconducting sheath and utilises a SQUID for the detection of current balance in the comparator windings.[15] With a later improved version of the superconducting current comparator, current ratio errors were reduced to less than 5×10^{-10}. In a fully cryogenic Josephson-effect voltage standard developed later, the superconducting current comparator was used for the calibration of resistance ratios.[16] Work with this equipment corroborated the results obtained with the original standard.

Harvey's work on the application of superconducting technology to electrical measurements was recognised in 1986 by the Morris E. Leeds Award of the Institute of Electrical and Electronic Engineers.

Quantised Hall Resistance

In 1981, work was started in the Laboratory by Dr B.W. Ricketts on the possibility of developing a resistance standard based on quantised Hall resistances.[17] It was shown by K. von Klitzing in Germany that, in some semiconductor devices at liquid helium temperatures, the Hall resistance varies with the magnetic field in such a way that there are intervals of flux density in which the Hall resistance is constant. It was shown theoretically that these "quantised Hall resistances" should be very close in value to sub-

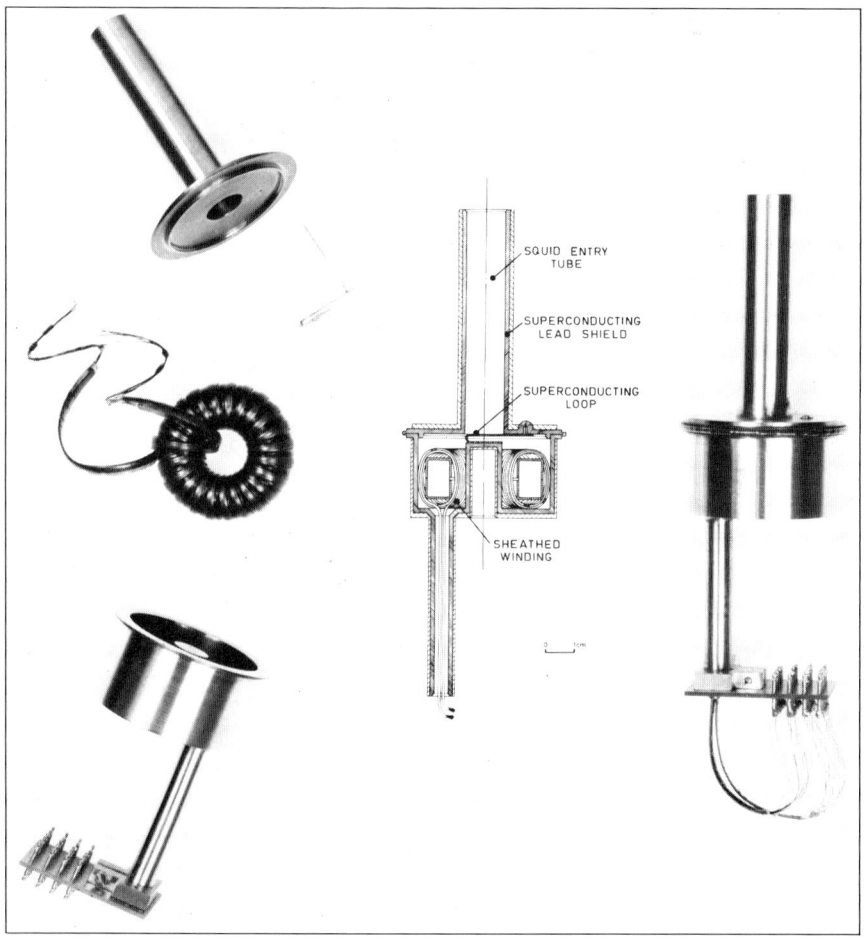

Superconducting current comparator showing design (centre), components (left) and assembled transformer (right).

multiples of h/e^2, where h is Planck's constant and e is the electron charge. Ricketts developed a measurement system for the precise comparison of quantised Hall resistances and very stable 1 Ω resistors with values derived from the calculable capacitor.[17] A special Hamon-type build-up resistor devised by Mr G.W. Small was used in the comparison of the 1 Ω resistors with room temperature resistors of a nominal value equal to one of the quantised Hall resistances (6453.2 Ω).[19]

These investigations gave a new value in SI units of the quantity h/e^2, which agreed within 2×10^{-7} with values obtained in other laboratories by quite independent methods. This confirmed that, as long as certain experimental requirements are satisfied, the quantised Hall resistances are independent of material properties, the dimensions of the semiconductor device and the values of parameters such as temperature and magnetic field. It is probable that devices based on quantised Hall resistances will be adopted as the preferred means of maintaining resistance standards after 1990. In late 1988, the Consultative Committee on Electricity will recommend to the International Committee of Weights and Measures a conventional "best value" for the quantity h/e^2.

The comparison of the absolute volt with the maintained volt based on the Josephson effect allows a determination of the value of the quantity $2e/h$ in SI units. This value has been combined with the value of h/e^2 obtained from the quantised Hall resistance measurements to calculate revised values for e and h.[20] NML is one of the few laboratories in which determinations of both $2e/h$ and h/e^2 have been made with sufficient accuracy to contribute significantly to electrical metrology and the determination of these fundamental physical constants.

Re-definition of the Candela

During World War 2, Dr R.G. Giovanelli established in the Laboratory a range of facilities for photometry, the measurements being based on secondary standard lamps that had been calibrated at the UK National Physical Laboratory. It was still the Laboratory's policy in the 1960s to rely on imported standards rather than to realise the primary photometric standard locally. At that time, the candela was defined by reference to the primary standard, a luminous blackbody radiator at the freezing point of platinum (about 2042 K), its luminance being 600 000 candela per square metre. It was a difficult standard to realise and few laboratories set up the necessary facilities.

During the 1960s, the Laboratory made many contributions to the related field of optical radiometry, in which optical radiation is measured in terms of the SI unit of power, the watt. The backwardness of this area of metrology at the time was indicated by a long-standing disagreement of about 2% between the experimental and theoretical values for the Stefan-Boltzmann constant, which relates the power radiated by a black body to its temperature. In 1971, Dr W.R. Blevin and Mr W.J. Brown completed a new determination of this constant, based on the use of an absolute radiometer to measure *in vacuo* the radiance of a large cavity radiator of graphite at the freezing point of gold[21], and resolved the disagreement.

Blevin's radiometric experience led him to the view that photometric units should be derived from radiometric measurements and thus related directly

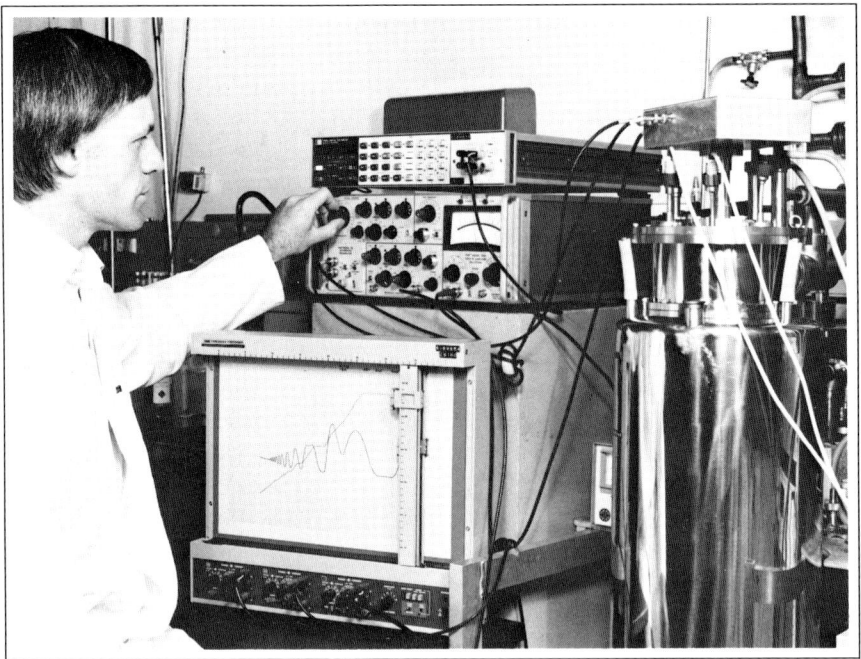

Dr B.W. Ricketts performing measurements for the development of a resistance standard based on the quantised Hall resistance.

to the watt rather than being based on a primary standard of light. With Brown and Mr J.E. Shaw, he demonstrated the practicality of this approach experimentally. The one major difficulty was that the definition of the candela, the base unit for photometry, at the time led to an uncertainty of about 2% in the relation between the photometric units and the watt. This arose mainly from the uncertainty of the freezing point of platinum. Blevin concluded that the candela should be re-defined by international agreement so as to give an explicit numerical relation between the candela and the watt, the numerical factor being chosen to maintain continuity with the old definition. He accepted an invitation to spend 1973 at the US National Bureau of Standards as a consultant and persuaded the Bureau to join him in seeking such a re-definition.[22]

In 1975, NML and the Bureau jointly recommended to the Consultative Committee on Photometry and Radiometry (CCPR) of the International Committee of Weights and Measures that the candela should be defined on the basis suggested by Blevin, with an exact value ascribed to K_m, the constant that relates the photometric units to the watt for monochromatic radiation of wavelength 555 nm. This wavelength is in the yellow-green region of the spectrum where the relative spectral response of the eye is maximum, and corresponds closely to the frequency 540×10^{12} Hz. The proposal was accepted by the CCPR and in October 1979, the General Conference of Weights and Measures formally adopted the recommendation of the CCPR that the candela be re-defined as follows.

> The candela is the luminous intensity, in a given direction, of a source that emits monochromatic radiation of frequency 540×10^{12} hertz and that has a radiant intensity in that direction of $(1/683)$ watt per steradian.

The change in the definition of the candela led to a much greater effort in photometry in many national standards laboratories, and the number of laboratories to realise the photometric units in terms of their definitions had doubled by 1985. Most of the realisations were based on measurements with absolute detectors of radiation rather than on a high-temperature blackbody source. Laboratories were attracted by the scope for applying the radiometric techniques to a wide range of other applications.

Fifteen national laboratories intercompared their new realisations of the candela in 1986 and the standard error of the mean of the results was found to be 0.15%. In 1987, the values attributed to the photometric standard lamps maintained by the BIPM were adjusted to conform with the mean result of the intercomparison and it was reported at the 18th General Conference of Weights and Measures that the advantages of the new definition of the candela had already been confirmed. The candela realised and maintained at NML agrees with the international mean to better than 0.1%.

Temperature Measurement

Among the standards brought back to the National Standards Laboratory by the scientists from the Laboratory who worked in the United Kingdom National Physical Laboratory in 1939 and 1940 were some that made it possible to set up a temperature scale. This was undertaken by Mr A.F.A. Harper. In 1940, when he returned to the Laboratory, temperature measurement was based on the International Temperature Scale (ITS 27) adopted by the General Conference of Weights and Measures in 1927. The standards brought back from NPL included a range of liquid-in-glass thermometers covering the range of temperatures from $-200°C$ to $600°C$, tungsten-strip lamps covering the range from $800°C$ to $2\ 300°C$ and samples of pure materials to set up the fixed points prescribed in the definition of ITS 27.

By the end of 1941, the Laboratory had a version of ITS 27 adequate for the immediate wartime needs for calibration. After the war, work was undertaken on the development of the scale over its entire range. Attention was given first to the development of improved platinum-resistance thermometers, particularly for use at very low temperatures. In 1950, a helium liquefier was manufactured and produced liquid helium for the first time in Australia. This made it possible for the Laboratory to initiate work on the measurement of very low temperatures.

By the early 1960s, the International Practical Temperature Scale of 1948 (IPTS 48), which replaced ITS 27, had been realised in the Laboratory by Mr J.V. McAllan in the range of platinum thermometry[23], Mr J. Middlehurst and Mr T.P. Jones in the thermocouple range, and by Jones in the range covered by visual optical pyrometry.[24] An international intercomparison of visual optical pyrometry scales showed that the NSL scale agreed well with those of other major laboratories.

During the 1960s, a photoelectric pyrometer was developed by Jones and Middlehurst. The replacement of optical pyrometry by this instrument led to a substantial improvement in the accuracy of realisation of the IPTS above the freezing point of gold and the Laboratory was able to contribute significantly to the evidence that led to the introduction of the International Practical Temperature Scale of 1968 (IPTS 68).

At the time of the introduction of IPTS 68, no national laboratory had satisfactorily realised the low-temperature part of the range. After the introduction of the new scale, Mr W.R.G. Kemp, Dr R.C. Kemp, Dr L.E. Besley and others in the Laboratory investigated the seven defining fixed points in the scale below 0°C (273.15 K). They developed techniques using flow cryostats which made the realisation of these fixed points much easier and improved their reproducibility.

Intercomparisons of the temperature scales of several national laboratories have shown that there are serious deficiencies in the IPTS 68 itself, especially below 30 K. There are differences of as much as 10 mK between IPTS 68 and thermodynamic temperatures.

With the aim of improving the accuracy of measurement of low temperatures, Kemp, Kemp and Besley developed a gas thermometer based on flow cryostat techniques. Work with this instrument confirmed that there are significant errors in IPTS 68 and provided a sound basis for an improved scale. New methods for interpolation between the fixed points below 273.15 K, much easier to use than those in IPTS 68, were also developed.[25]

For many years, there has been international cooperation in investigations of possible differences between IPTS 68 and thermodynamic temperatures

Comparison of optical pyrometer and platinum resistance thermometer using a heat pipe.

above 0°C. In the Laboratory, investigations by McAllan and Mr J.J. Connolly have extended the range of use of platinum-resistance thermometers up to the freezing point of silver (962°C) and Jones and Mr J. Tapping have extended the range of the Laboratory's photoelectric pyrometer down beyond this temperature.[26] This work has made it possible to develop interpolation procedures for the use of platinum thermometers up to 962°C. The results of the work will be used in the formulation of the revised version of the IPTS expected to be adopted in 1990.

Gravitational Acceleration

In 1971, an absolute determination of the acceleration of gravity by Mr G.A. Bell, Dr D.L.H. Gibbings and Mr J.B. Patterson was completed. This was the first absolute determination in the Southern Hemisphere. A body in the form of a corner cube reflector was projected upwards in a vacuum and the time intervals between successive passages through two horizontal planes were measured. The separation of the planes was measured interferometrically and the passage of the reflector was detected by means of interference in white light. The uncertainty of the determination was estimated to be not more than 1 in 10^7.

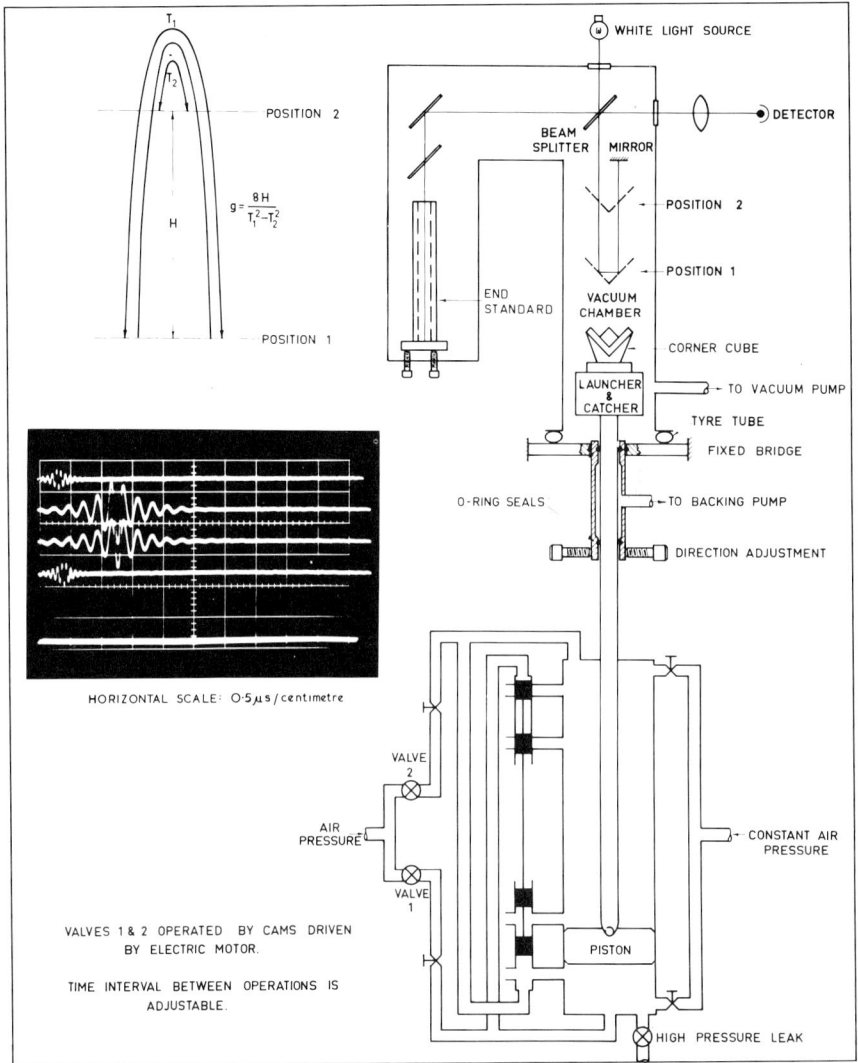

Schematic of the absolute measurement of gravitational acceleration.

Psychrometry

The Laboratory has also contributed to the work of other international scientific bodies. An example is the development of a psychrometer that has been adopted by the World Meteorological Organization (WMO) as the international reference standard instrument for meteorological humidity measurement.

Work on humidity measurement and control was started during World War 2 in connection with investigations into the failure of military equipment under tropical conditions. After the war, investigations on the requirements for accurate humidity measurement were continued. The development of a reference psychrometer for meteorological use was recommended by the Working Group on Hygrometry of the World Meteorological Organization in 1963. In 1965, a theoretical and experimental study of psychrometry was started in the Laboratory by Dr R.G. Wylie. In parallel with this, work was undertaken on the development of a reference psychrometer.

The instrument developed by Wylie and Mr T. Lalas was tested extensively in Australia and overseas and a report on its performance was presented to the meeting of the WMO Commission for Instruments and Methods of Observation in Hamburg in August 1977. The Commission recommended to the WMO Executive Committee that the psychrometer be adopted as the official international reference instrument and the Committee adopted the recommendation.[27] In 1981, the WMO also adopted the instrument as the international reference standard for meteorological temperature measurement, with effect from the beginning of 1985.

Collaboration in the Asia-Pacific Region

In recent years, the Laboratory has been able to help in the development of standards facilities in developing countries in Asia and the Pacific region. Members of the staff have worked in laboratories being established in various countries or have helped to introduce expertise in new fields in existing laboratories.

In 1977, the Commonwealth Science Council established the CSC Regional (Asia/Pacific) Metrology Programme, with the aim of improving and extending the national measurement services in Commonwealth countries in the region. About the same time, several other regional metrology projects, funded by various national and international agencies, were set up. To make the best use of the funds and resources available, these schemes were amalgamated in September 1980 to establish an Asia-Pacific Metrology Programme, initially involving seventeen nations. It is based on the idea that nations in the region with well-established national measurement systems can give substantial help to nations where such systems are being developed.

From September 1980 until September 1983, the Regional Coordinator of the Programme was Mr T.P. Jones, a member of the staff of the National Measurement Laboratory. The main activities under the Programme have been information transfer on measurement systems, training of staff, calibration and intercomparison of standards and assessment of

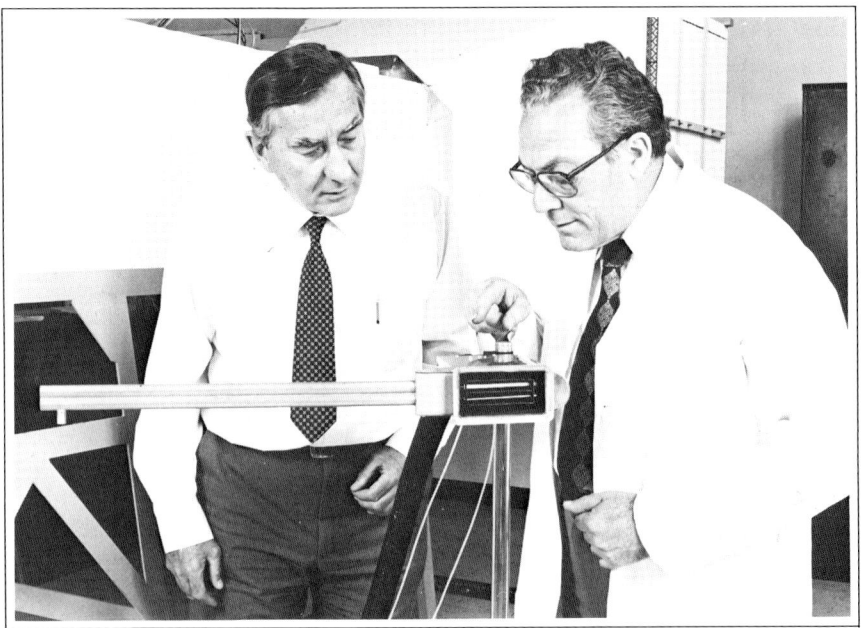

Dr R.G. Wylie and Mr T. Lalas discuss a point concerning the reference psychrometer which they developed for the World Meteorological Organization. The particular form shown, which uses mercury-in-glass thermometers, is intended for use by under-developed countries. The atmosphere is drawn into the rectangular opening at a set rate over wet and dry temperature sensors which are contained in long thin-walled stainless-steel tubes.

measurement capability. Several conferences have been held, including a Regional Workshop on Metrology for Developing Countries held at the Laboratory from 30 August to 10 September 1982. The Laboratory has calibrated standards for many of the countries in the region and has provided coordinators for several intercomparisons of standards. It has been greatly assisted in its participation in the Programme by funds provided by the Australian Development Assistance Bureau of the Department of Foreign Affairs.

Notes and References

1. Bruce, C.F., *J. Sci. Instrum.*, **33,** 478 (1956)

2. Bruce, C.F., and Ciddor, P.E., *J. Opt. Soc. Amer.*, **50,** 295 (1960); Ciddor, P.E., *Opt. Acta*, **7,** 399 (1960).

3. Bruce, C.F., *Opt. Acta*, **4,** 128 (1957).

4.   Thompson, A.M., and Lampard, D.E., *Nature,* **177,** 888 (1956).

5.   Thompson, A.M., *Proc. IEEE,* **106 B,** 307 (1959);
     Clothier, W.K., *Metrologia,* **1,** 4 (1965).

6.   Thompson, A.M., *Metrologia,* **4,** 1 (1968).

7.   Hamon, B.V., *J. Sci. Instrum.,* **31,** 450 (1954).

8.   Press Release, *Our Atomic – Electronic World,* 11 December 1957, on the occasion of the 18th Annual Dinner Meeting of the 210 Associates Inc., Boston, Massachusetts.

9.   Small, G.W., *IEEE Trans. Instrum. Meas.,* **IM-36,** 190 (1987).

10. Clothier, W.K., *Metrologia,* **1,** 35 (1965).

11. Sloggett, G.J. *et al., Digest, Conference on Precise Electrical Measurement,* 35 (1984); *IEEE Trans. Instrum. Meas.,* **IM-34,** 187 (1985).

12. In 1962, B.D. Josephson, working in the United Kingdom, predicted that an emf V established across a weak link between two superconductors would result in the generation of an alternating current with a frequency of $2e / h \times V$, where e is the electron charge and h is Planck's constant.

13. Harvey, I.K., Macfarlane, J.C., and Frenkel, R.B., *Metrologia,* **8,** 114 (1972).

14. A SQUID is a very sensitive detector of magnetic fields. The name is an acronym from superconducting quantum interference device.

15. Harvey, I.K., *Rev. Sci. Instrum.,* **43,** 1626 (1972).

16. Harvey, I.K., *Metrologia,* **12,** 47 (1976).

17. A Hall voltage is developed in a current-carrying metal or semiconductor when a magnetic field is applied at right angles to the direction of current flow. The Hall resistance is the ratio of the Hall voltage to the current.

18. Ricketts, B.W., and Cage, M.E., *IEEE Trans. Instrum. Meas.,* **IM-36,** 245 (1987).

19. Small, G.W., *IEEE Trans. Instrum. Meas.,* **IM-32,** 446 (1983).

20. Sloggett, G.J., Clothier, W.K., and Ricketts, B.W., *Phys. Rev. Lett.,* **57,** 3237 (1986).

21. Blevin, W.R., and Brown, W.J., *Metrologia,* **7,** 15 (1971).

22. Blevin, W.R., and Steiner, R., *Metrologia,* **11,** 97 (1975).

23. McAllan, J.V., *Conf. de Comité Consultative de Thermometrie, 6th Session 1962,* 52 (1962).

24. Jones, T.P., *Metrologia,* **4,** 80 (1968).

25.   Kemp, R.C., Kemp, W.R.G., and Besley, L.M., *Metrologia*, **23,** 61 (1986/7).

26.   Jones, T.P., and Tapping, J., *Metrologia*, **8,** 4 (1972).

27.   Wylie, R.G., and Lalas, T., *The WMO Reference Psychrometer*, CSIRO (1981).

Contributions to International Science

The Secondary Industries Testing and Research Committee in 1937 recommended that the work essential for the maintenance of standards and calibration facilities in the proposed standards laboratory should be accompanied by related research. The realisation of this concept was delayed by the need for concentration on short-term problems during World War 2. At the end of the war, it became possible to give attention to longer-term research. In addition to research specifically directed at the development of improved standards and measuring techniques, research in other areas of physics and engineering utilising the special facilities and skills of a standards laboratory or complementing these skills was initiated. Some of this research is described in this chapter.

Some research activities started in the Laboratory during and soon after the war were continued for only a short time. Work on the physics of wool fibres was transferred to the Physics and Engineering Unit of the Wool Textile Research Laboratories of CSIRO when they were established in 1949. In the immediate post-war years, research related to the development of equipment for the linear acceleration of elementary particles was undertaken in the Division of Physics in collaboration with a group in the Division of Radiophysics. Work in the Laboratory in atomic physics was discontinued after 1948.

Dielectric Absorption

The investigation of the failure of electrical equipment under tropical conditions during World War 2 brought those engaged in this work into contact with the literature on the dielectric properties of solids and liquids. They realised that progress in understanding of dielectrics required more thorough measurements on better characterised materials. It was decided that research on dielectric properties should be undertaken by a multi-disciplinary group led by Dr R.J. Meakins in parallel with the development of capability in the measurement of the electrical properties of materials.

There was general agreement before the war that dielectric absorption in liquids was due to the rotation of dipoles but there was only limited evidence that this was the case in solids. One class of solids, long-chain aliphatic compounds, had been investigated in the United Kingdom with the aim of finding why the dielectric properties of the wax used to impregnate paper capacitors deteriorated when it was heated. The initial work undertaken in the Laboratory involved the preparation of a wide range of long-chain aliphatic compounds of high purity and the development of equipment for measuring dielectric properties. While some measuring equipment was available commercially, it was necessary, in order to cover the frequency and temperature ranges involved, to design and construct instruments, with the cooperation of scientists concerned with electrical standards in the Laboratory.

It was discovered that dielectric absorption due to dipole rotation in these compounds was more complex than expected. In some instances, more than one absorption region was found. The major finding made during the 1950s, was that in most cases, dielectric absorption is not an intrinsic property as had been assumed, but is only present if there are crystal imperfections due either to chemical impurities or physical imperfections caused by plastic deformation.[1] The nature of impurities that could make molecular rotation possible was determined. Although it was known that crystal defects were important in metals and ionic crystals, this was an early recognition of the importance of defects in molecular crystals.

At about the same time, work was started on the use of dielectric absorption measurements in the study of defects in the crystalline structure of alkali halides. The alkali halides have relatively simple crystalline structures suitable for experiments to test theoretical concepts of general relevance in solids in which the motion of atoms or ions within the crystal structure is of technological importance. Measurements in the Laboratory have provided definitive information about the mobility of ions in these crystals. Dr J.S. Dryden and Dr J.S. Cook pioneered the study of clustering of defects in ionic materials[2] and were able to study the relations between aggregation of defects and physical properties such as hardness, thermoluminescence, and optical emission and absorption. The studies have been extended to other ionic solids in which dielectric absorption is more complex than in the alkali halides.

Other research on liquids and solids has included work on the electric properties of heterogeneous materials and ferroelectric transitions and the first measurements of dipole relaxation due to internal rotation in liquids. In recent years, the study of heterogeneous materials has been extended to rocks to provide background information for geophysical prospecting.

Magnetics Research

The Laboratory provided a measurement service on the magnetic properties of materials, particularly at power frequencies, from 1947. Research on magnetic materials did not start until 1967, when studies on

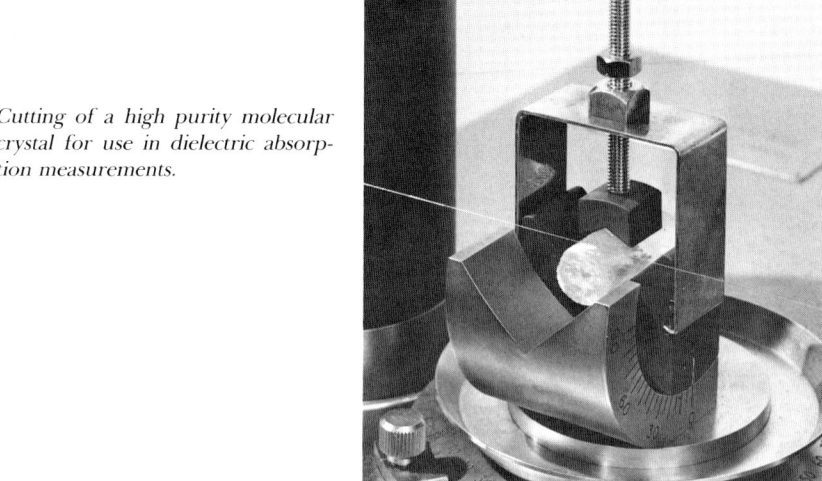

Cutting of a high purity molecular crystal for use in dielectric absorption measurements.

intermetallic compounds between rare earth and other metals were initiated by Dr G.J. Bowden and were continued by Dr R.K. Day and Dr J.B. Dunlop. These materials are of scientific and technological importance, intermetallic compounds of this kind being the most powerful magnetic materials in commercial use.

Among the techniques used to investigate the complex magnetic interactions within these compounds was Mossbauer spectroscopy, used to determine the magnetic fields acting at different crystallographic sites. With this technique, the nature of the transitions in the magnetic properties of several intermetallic compounds was determined.[3]

Glassy Metals

Some alloys, if quenched rapidly from a molten state, can be produced in a non-crystalline form. In this form, they are known as glassy metals and have properties strikingly different from those of the same alloys in their normal state. Glassy metals combine great strength with high ductility. Some glassy metals based on iron have desirable magnetic properties and a facility was established by Day and Dunlop in 1981 to prepare glassy metal ribbons of these and other alloys. It has been shown for the first time that alloys of iron and scandium can be produced in glassy form[4] and that the glassy forms have technologically interesting properties. Superconducting transitions in another range of glassy metals have also been studied.

Properties of Solids at Low Temperatures

At the end of World War 2, it was decided that facilities for achieving very low temperatures should be set up in the Laboratory. Dr G.H. Briggs, Chief of the Division of Physics, was able to obtain considerable information on the liquefaction of helium in the United States and to purchase some equipment. The construction of a helium liquefier was undertaken by Mr A.F.A. Harper and Mr W.R.G. Kemp, with members of the workshop staff. In June 1950, the liquefier, the first in Australia, was brought into operation in the Laboratory by Kemp. It supplied the needs of the Laboratory for 15 years before it was replaced by a larger commercial machine. This was probably the only Collins-type liquefier other than those built by Collins himself at Massachusetts Institute of Technology or by Arthur D. Little Inc. that operated successfully.

The availability of liquid helium opened the way both for the development of low-temperature-measuring capability and for research on materials at low temperatures. This was expected to provide information on the structural and other factors that affect physical properties, measurements at very low temperatures allowing study of phenomena that are obscured by thermal lattice vibrations at higher temperatures. There was also a need for more precise information on the properties of materials of importance in technology and in scientific research, and of reference materials used for instrument calibration.

Work on the temperature-dependence of heat and electric conduction of simple metals such as gold, copper and silver was started in 1950 by Dr G.K. White and Dr P.G. Klemens.[5] The work was extended to binary alloy systems to study the mechanism of heat conduction and the effects of lattice dislocations and point defects. More recently, the Laboratory has collaborated with several overseas laboratories and the Committee on Data for Science and Technology (CODATA) in establishing reliable values for the thermal conductivity of standard reference materials produced by the US National Bureau of Standards.

In 1955, Dr J.A. Rayne began work on the heat capacity of metals at liquid helium temperatures and later, White, with Dr J.G. Collins and Mr J.A. Birch, made measurements on silver-rich alloys, iron-nickel alloys, vitreous silica, sodium silicate glasses and alkali halides.[6]

Work on thermal expansion began in 1959. White made use of equipment and techniques developed in the Laboratory by A.M. Thompson for the

The Laboratory's helium liquifying facility (centre left)
with cryogenic experiment in progress.

measurement of very small capacitances, to make the necessary differential
length measurements. These investigations provided information on the
relative contributions to thermal expansion of lattice vibrations, electrons
and magnetic interactions. Subsequently, measurements have been made
on a wide range of metals, insulators and semiconductors.

Thermoelectric Power

Thermoelectric power is also an important property of metals and
semiconductors. It is a measure of the voltage generated when heat flows
through a material. Thermoelectricity provides the basis for thermocouples
and thermoelectric cooling devices. In 1976, Dr R.B. Roberts made the first
direct measurements between 17 K and 450 K of the Thomson heat of
lead.[7] The Thomson heat of a material is related to the thermoelectric
power, being the additional, reversible heat flow generated in a material
subjected to simultaneous electrical and thermal gradients. A new
thermoelectric power scale for lead was calculated from these
measurements. Subsequently measurements were made on lead at
temperatures up to its melting point and on copper up to 850 K. Recent

work in collaboration with the Italian Istituto di Metrologia has provided accurate information on the thermoelectric power of platinum and tungsten at temperatures up to 1330°C.

Interferometry

Shortly after the war, the need for better methods for testing microscope objectives led Dr W.H. Steel to construct an interferometer. Over the following years, he and other research workers in the Laboratory developed interferometric instruments and techniques. Various special purpose interferometers were constructed. In 1962, Dr J.V. Ramsay overcame one of the most serious disadvantages of Fabry-Perot interferometers with a system of servo-control of the positions of the optical elements. Interferometers of this type depend on the reflection of light back and forwards between two flat, parallel glass plates. Interference of the light rays makes it possible to produce an output consisting of light within a very narrow range of wavelengths. The problem had always been to maintain the plates parallel and at a fixed spacing while observations were made over reasonable periods. Ramsay's design made a great improvement in stability possible and later, several instruments were made commercially by Scientific Optical Laboratories of Australia Pty. Ltd., of Adelaide.

In 1967, Dr Steel reviewed developments in interferometry in the book "Interferometry", published in the Cambridge Monographs on Physics series, and produced a second edition in 1983.[8]

Properties of Gases and Gas-Vapour Mixtures

In the mid-1960s, Dr R.G. Wylie developed a plan for the accurate measurement of the PVT properties of gases at pressures up to about 1000 MPa (approximately 10 000 atmospheres). The object was to obtain data from which information on the intermolecular forces at high densities could be derived.

For these investigations, improvements in high-pressure measurement were needed. Mr A.R. Beavitt studied the properties of the manganin used in electrical-resistance pressure gauges and in 1969 showed how the material should be used for best results. Dr E.C. Morris used the results to establish an accurate pressure scale based on pressure-balance calibrations at moderate pressures and on the melting pressure of mercury at 0°C. He then determined the melting curve of mercury for pressures up to 750 MPa.[9] This determination, published in 1978 and confirmed by work at the US National Bureau of Standards, established a new and much more accurate scale for the measurement of high pressures.

Measurement of the PVT properties of gases at high pressures. The main apparatus, behind the safety panel operates at pressures up to 1400 MPa.

In the 1970s, Wylie devised an improved method of determining PVT properties at high pressures, gaining important advantages by using a thin lining of silver in the PVT vessel. With this method, Morris and Wylie greatly extended the range and accuracy of the data available for argon and nitrogen.[10] Morris further extended the data for argon and later applied the method to methane. This series of investigations thus provided extensive and accurate new data for a monatomic, a diatomic and a polyatomic molecule.

The equilibrium composition of gas-vapour mixtures over water for air and some other gases have been measured by Wylie and Mr R. Fisher at various temperatures and at pressures up to 15 MPa. From the results, the intermolecular forces in the mixtures, the thermodynamic properties of the mixtures and other properties of water vapour in gases at high pressures can be calculated. These results also make possible the convenient generation of gas streams of known water content for the calibration of humidity-measuring instruments.

Solar Physics

Research on the physics of the outer layers of the Sun was started in the Laboratory by Dr R.G. Giovanelli in 1946. An initial theoretical study of chromospheric flares led to an observational program, starting at the Laboratory but later carried out at Fleurs, about 50 kilometres west of Sydney, and from the mid-1960s at Culgoora, in northern New South Wales.

In 1951, observations were started with a spectroheliograph constructed in the Laboratory. A 127 mm refracting telescope with electronic guidance was fitted with a Lyot-type filter giving a waveband of 0.06 nm centred on the H_α line. Exposures were made at half-minute intervals. In 1957, a high-resolution photoheliograph was installed at Fleurs. It was used to produce sequences of photographs of selected portions of the solar photosphere.[11] In 1959, a seeing monitor was installed. This was a device in which the light intensities of opposite edges of an image of the Sun were compared photo-electrically so that the heliograph could be triggered at times of good seeing.

Observations with this equipment led to significant increases in the understanding of the granulation in the photosphere itself and in sunspots and faculae, which are areas of higher brightness than the surrounding photosphere. In the period from May 1957 to June 1960, a period that included the intense solar maximum of 1957-58, some fifty different groups of sunspots were photographed, about 100 000 photographs being obtained. The results of the analysis of these observations were presented in the book "Sunspots", by Dr R.J. Bray and Mr R.E. Loughhead, which was published in the International Astrophysics Series in 1964.[12]

In 1960, Giovanelli, in cooperation with Dr W.H. Steel and Mr R.N. Smartt, completed the construction of a birefringent filter transmitting a bandwidth of 0.0125 nm. With this, it was possible to make exposures at wavelengths just below and just above the central wavelength of the H_α line. By measuring the Doppler shifts due to line-of-sight velocities in the chromosphere, the distribution of these velocities over the Sun's surface could be studied. This filter was first installed on a 127 mm telescope at Fleurs and used by Dr J.M. Beckers in an important series of observations over large areas of the Sun's surface.

In 1963, it was decided that the Laboratory, in conjunction with the CSIRO Division of Radiophysics, would set up a radio and optical solar observatory at Culgoora, near Narrabri, about 560 km north west of Sydney. The first installation, during 1964, was of a 127 mm flare patrol telescope for use in an international collaborative program. The telescope came into routine use in January 1965. Construction of a new 300 mm chromospheric telescope was also started and it was brought into use in 1967.[13]

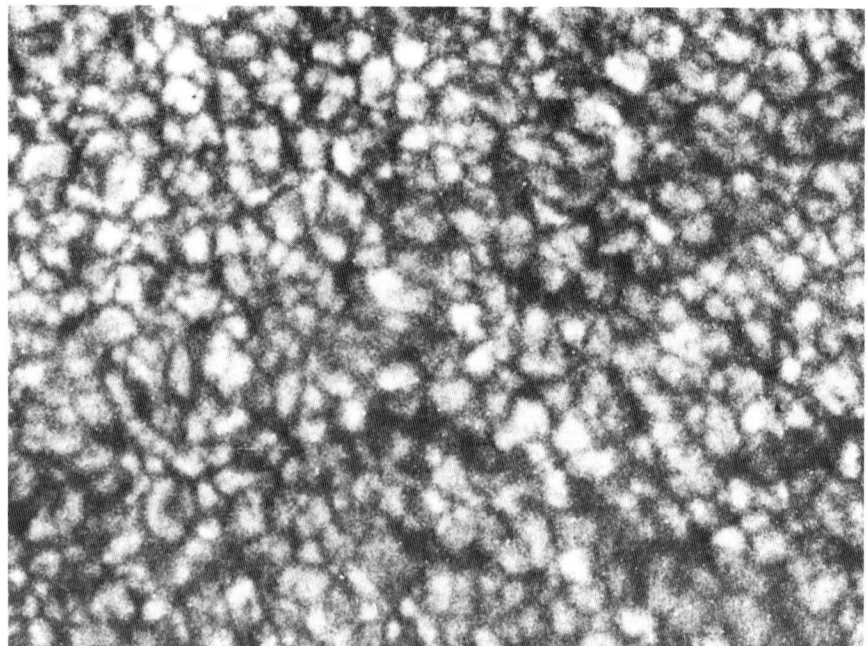

Solar granulation photographed with the 300 mm telescope of the CSIRO Solar Observatory, Culgoora, NSW. Each granule represents the top of a rising column of hot gas.

An account of studies on the solar granulation was published in the International Astrophysics Series in 1967 in the book "The Solar Granulation" by Bray and Loughhead,[14] a second edition of which appeared in 1984.

In 1969, the 0.0125 nm birefringent filter was installed on the 300 mm chromospheric telescope and at the same time equipped with computer control of its tuning mechanism. With a 0.1 nm Halle filter ahead of the 0.0125 nm filter, photographs of very good quality were obtained and used to study a variety of quiet- and active-region phenomena in the chromosphere.[15] A further book by Bray and Loughhead in the International Astrophysical Series, "The Solar Chromosphere", was published in 1974.[16]

Soon after the establishment of the Culgoora observatory, work was started on the development of a cinemagnetograph, with the aim of investigating the configuration of magnetic fields on the Sun by means of high-resolution time-lapse photography. It consisted essentially of a filter with a bandwidth of about 0.005 nm, arranged so as to transmit simultaneously two

Universal filter shown mounted on the 300 mm telescope at Culgoora. One of the 3 interferometers has been removed for on-site adjustment.

orthogonally polarised bands of slightly differing wavelengths, and an electronic image subtractor. The filter was based on a series of three Fabry-Perot interferometers with a sheet of mica of appropriate thickness in the optical path.[17]

While some useful observations were made with this equipment, severe problems were experienced in maintaining stable settings of the interferometers. In 1975, consideration was given to the design and construction of a new universal filter. The aim was to retain the band-width of 0.005 nm, but provide for computer-controlled selection of any one of ten spectral lines with fine-tuning across any one of them. The design was again based on the use of three Fabry-Perot interferometers in series.[18]

The achievement of the desired resolution, finesse and stability was extremely difficult and the filter was not ready for final laboratory testing until 1984. It was successfully installed and tested on the 300 mm telescope at Culgoora during 1985 and 1986. In August 1986, however, following the recommendations of the Goldsmid Committee, the CSIRO Executive decided that solar physics research in the Laboratory should be discontinued, and the optical solar observatory was closed in June 1987.

References

1.   Welsh, H.K., *Trans. Faraday Soc.*, **55,** 52 (1959).

2.   Cook, J.S., and Dryden, J.S., *Proc. Phys. Soc.,* **80,** 479 (1962).

3.   Day, R.K., and Bowden, G.J., *J. Phys. F,***7,** 191 (1977).

4.   Day, R.K., Dunlop, J.B., Foley, C.P., Ghafari, M., and Pask, H., *Solid State Commun.,* **56,** 843 (1985).

5.   White, G.K., *Proc. Phys. Soc.,* **A66,** 559 (1953).

6.   Birch, J.A., *J. Phys. C,* **8,** 1043 (1975).

7.   Roberts, R.B., *Philos. Mag.,* **36,** 91 (1977).

8.   Steel. W.H., *Interferometry,* Cambridge University Press, 1st Ed. Cambridge (1967), 2nd Ed. Cambridge (1983).

9.   Morris, E.C., *Metrologia,* **14,** 105 (1978).

10. Morris, E.C., and Wylie, R.G., *J. Chem. Phys.,* **73,** 1359 (1980); **79,** 2982 (1983).

11. Loughhead, R.E., and Burgess, V.R., *Aust. J. Phys.,* **11,** 35 (1958).

12. Bray, R.J., and Loughhead, R.E., *Sunspots,* Chapman and Hall, London (1964).

13. Loughhead, R.E., Bray, R.J., Tappere, E.J., and Winter, J.G., *Sol. Phys.,* **4,** 185 (1968).

14. Bray, R.J., and Loughhead, R.E., *The Solar Granulation,* Chapman and Hall, London (1967), 2nd Ed. Cambridge (1984).

15. Loughhead, R.E., and Tappere, E.J., *Sol. Phys.,* **19,** 44 (1971).

16. Bray, R.J., and Loughhead, R.E., *The Solar Chromosphere,* Chapman and Hall, London (1974).

17. Ramsay, J.V., Kobler, H. and Mugridge, E.G.V., *Sol. Phys.,* **12,** 492 (1970).

18. Loughhead, R.E., Bray, R.J., and Brown, N., *Appl. Opt.,* **17,** 4115 (1978).

The Laboratory, Industry and the Community

The National Standards Laboratory, when it was established in 1938, was planned to be a basic part of the provision in CSIR for meeting the testing and research needs of industry in Australia. With the outbreak of World War 2 in September 1939, the newly established Laboratory was immediately faced with many calls for help, not only with standards and measurements, but also with a wide range of problems faced by manufacturing industry, government factories and the armed services in dealing with the new situation.

Meeting these demands and taking part in the Approved Test House scheme, set up jointly by the Laboratory and the Munitions Supply Laboratories of the Department of Munitions, brought the Laboratory into contact with many industrial establishments. Much of the demand was in the field of mechanical engineering and a small group led by Dr H.H. Davis, besides providing standards and calibrations for existing measuring instruments, was able to advise on the acquisition and installation of measuring and testing equipment, and to help in the training of operators. The Laboratory was also able to assist many firms and institutions in the establishment of equipment for electrical and other measurements.

After the war ended, many of the contacts that had been established led to continuing involvement of the Laboratory with industry as it adjusted to production for civilian needs. In the Division of Metrology, work related to production engineering continued, and in 1950, an Applied Mechanics Section, led by Mr C.A. Gladman, was formed. It undertook research concerned with the geometric analysis of engineering designs, the machining of metals and the measurement of machinability, as well as continuing to provide a calibration service for materials testing machines. When Gladman retired in 1970, the activities of the section were reviewed. It was concluded that it was desirable for its work to be conducted in an environment where there was interaction with metallurgists and metal physicists and, in 1972, it was transferred to the CSIRO Division of Tribophysics in Melbourne.

Tests and Measurements

The basic functions of the Laboratory, the maintenance of measurement standards and the provision of calibration services, continued but, with the development of the National Association of Testing Authorities from 1947 onwards, calibration of industrial measuring equipment has been progressively transferred to laboratories registered by NATA. The Laboratory, in its calibration work, has been increasingly occupied with the calibration of reference standards for NATA laboratories and for government bodies concerned with weights and measures administration.

The number of tests and measurements carried out in the Laboratory per year increased steadily for some years, reaching a level of around 1500 during the 1960s and 1970s, but has declined in more recent years. The numbers however do not give an accurate indication of the extent of activities of this kind in any year. As the ability of other laboratories to undertake the less demanding tasks has developed, those dealt with by the Laboratory have tended to be more complex and time-consuming.

In the year ending 30 June 1987, 992 tests and calibrations were carried out. Of these, more than half were for industrial firms, most of the others being for other government departments or instrumentalities, including other Divisions of CSIRO. As with other national standards laboratories, the fees charged are based on the assumption that the cost of the provision of the basic facilities and of the research necessary to develop adequate measurement capability should be regarded as a national investment, the charge for any measurement being based on the actual cost of making it. Over the period 1983-1987, the annual income from fees was approximately $400 000, which, on a population basis, compares well with fee income of standards laboratories in other countries. The fee structure has been reviewed recently and this has resulted in substantial increases as from 1 July 1987.

Cautious Collaboration

The Laboratory in its earlier years, along with other Divisions of CSIR, was cautious in dealing with requests from industry for help. It was realised that most members of its staff, while they were well qualified to undertake research in physics and engineering, did not have detailed knowledge of industrial processes, and in particular, of the technicalities of production in individual firms. CSIR policy was generally based on the assumption that its relatively limited resources would be best used if applied to basic research, producing information that could be applied to the solution of the problems of individual firms by technically qualified people within these firms.

The results of the research work in the Laboratory were generally published in scientific journals, but, as relatively few people capable of interpreting such information were employed in industry, the possibility that the Laboratory could give scientific assistance was often not recognised. There

Measuring the temperature of an industrial furnace using a thermocouple in a ceramic sheath. Photo: circa 1950.

were exceptions. One early instance of direct collaboration between industry and the Laboratory was the appointment in 1946 of Mrs L.E.R. Rogers by the Broken Hill Proprietary Co. Ltd. to work in the Division of Physics on the physics of solids.

The need for more effective contacts with industry also became apparent in other parts of CSIRO and, from the mid-1950s, increasing efforts were made to stimulate and facilitate the transfer of technology from the research laboratories to industry.

With the establishment in the Head Office of CSIRO of an Industrial Research Liaison Section in 1956, information on research in CSIRO laboratories that had potential for industrial application was brought to the attention of executives regularly in terms more readily comprehensible than formal scientific publications. Items concerning activities in the Laboratory were often included. Within the Laboratory, there was also increased effort to establish effective contacts with industry and to encourage the transfer of technology. "Open Days" were arranged to provide opportunity for people from industry to see the facilities of the Laboratory and to discuss their technical problems with members of the staff.

Increasing Industrial Emphasis

During the 1950s and 1960s, much of the effort in the Laboratory was devoted to the improvement of its standards and measurement capability. Contacts that arose through the standards and calibration activities of the Laboratory did often lead to the application of its special facilities and skills in the solution of problems in industry and in other research establishments.

In the 1970s, increasing attention was given to direct assistance to industry in relation both to the solution of production problems and to the development of new products and processes. The CSIRO-Secondary Industry Committee (Weber Committee) in 1972 and the Review Committee on the CSIRO National Standards Laboratory (Street Committee) in 1973 both recommended that, especially after the move to the new site at Lindfield, there should be increased effort to establish contacts with secondary industry and to develop collaborative research programs.

The move to the new site and the increased demand for calibrations associated with metrication limited the extent to which resources could be made available for industrial collaborative projects. Flexibility was further limited when economic restraints led to the imposition of staff ceilings, which made it impossible in many cases to make new appointments when experienced staff members retired. The total calibration demand was also increased by the transfer to the Laboratory of responsibility for high-level calibrations for the Department of Defence and the armed services.

In August 1977, the CSIRO Working Party on Assistance to Manufacturing Industry, with Dr W.R. Blevin, of the Laboratory, as Convener, stated in its report that "a considerable change of emphasis towards research of greater industrial relevance is now desirable for NML". It concluded that: "NML should reconsider the Laboratory's objectives, as a step towards increasing its assistance to manufacturing industry. It should concentrate on developing sizeable research projects clearly relevant to Australian industry, as a function complementary to its standards work and in order to realize the Laboratory's potential more fully. The present economic stringencies should not be allowed to delay this change of emphasis, even if a significant reduction of the present pure and standards research should prove necessary. NML should assume a much more active role in establishing appropriate contacts with industry".

In the Biennial Report of the Laboratory (now known as the Division of Applied Physics) for 1977-79, it was noted that "the move to the new site coincided with a turning point in the scientific program of the Division. Since the end of World War II, a considerable part of the effort in the Division had been necessarily devoted to the establishment of standards facilities. By the mid-1970s, the Division had reached the point where it was well equipped to deal with almost all of the regular high-level calibration requirements of Australian industry and the community, with the exception of force standards. It became possible, approximately at the time of the move, for some of the resources of the Division to be diverted to other activities and there has been an increasing emphasis on research relating directly to problems of Australian manufacturing industry".

It was reported that "one immediate consequence [of the recommendations of the Working Party] was the establishment of an Industry Committee with a full-time Executive Officer to stimulate initiatives relating to industry and to coordinate the relevant activities."

By mid-1981, the CSIRO Executive had endorsed most of the recommendations of the Review Committee on the National Measurement Laboratory (Philip Committee) and Dr J.J. Lowke had been appointed as Chief. In the Biennial Report for 1979-81, Dr Lowke recorded that, where standards work had been approximately two-thirds of the work of the Laboratory, activities of this kind "now occupy only one-half of the total effort of the Division". "Much has been written on the need for CSIRO to make an increased contribution to manufacturing industry in Australia", he wrote. "Manufacturing industry generally uses imported technology and sells under a protective tariff structure. The key to improving this situation is local research. Innovation need not necessarily result in a completely new industry. Any improvements in a stage of manufacture or the detection and prevention of faults which interrupt the manufacturing process make the industry more viable".

The Applied Physics Industrial Program

In October 1983, the Applied Physics Industrial Program was announced. The program was based on the idea of appointing scientists for terms of up to three years specifically for the development of new products or for improving the efficiency of manufacturing processes. In particular, the intention was to provide for scientists from firms in industry to work in the Laboratory and return to their firms on completion of their projects. A joint industry–CSIRO committee was set up to assess proposals and to select those that would be followed up. CSIRO allocated $200 000 for the scheme and further funding from participating firms was expected.

Advertisements inviting proposals were issued in October 1983, with a closing date of 19 November. Many inquiries resulted and nineteen firm proposals were received by the closing date. Because of the limitation of resources, only eight projects were accepted, five being expected to be completed within a year and the other three in three years. Collaborators included both large and small firms and, in at least one case, a consortium of firms. Further advertisements were published early in 1985. Altogether, 18 projects have been approved.

In November 1984, CSIRO announced the establishment of SIROTECH, a non-profit company set up to assist in the transfer of technology from CSIRO Divisions to industry. The company functions to bring CSIRO staff members into contact with firms in cases where collaboration might be possible, providing expertise in relation to patents and licences, and taking part in negotiations in connection with collaborative or other commercial agreements. The Laboratory has used the services of SIROTECH in negotiating several recent collaborative agreements.

The amendment of the Science and Industry Research Act in 1986 and the consequent changes in the structure of CSIRO led to still greater emphasis on research aimed at producing short-term benefits to Australian industry. The range of activities involving interaction with industry is very large and it is not feasible to describe more than a few examples. The solution of the problems dealt with in these activities generally requires research leading to the acquisition of new knowledge, but the Laboratory is also able to assist, often with the cooperation of colleagues in overseas laboratories, in the application of scientific and technical information from other sources. Some collaborative activities, including projects that involve collaboration over several years, cannot be discussed at this stage because of considerations of commercial secrecy.

Collaboration Involving Special Measurement Capability

An early example of the application of the unusual measurement capability of the Laboratory was in the installation of rolling mills at Port Kembla in 1956. The six pairs of rolls in a hot mill at the plant of Australian Iron and Steel Pty. Ltd. had to be mounted so that any alignment error would be no more than one hundredth of an inch in the overall length of 90 feet. It was also necessary for the rolls to be as nearly parallel as possible. Mr M.J. Puttock and Mr J.W. Bell devised optical techniques that had the necessary sensitivity. A cold mill at Lysaghts Works Pty. Ltd., although having only four sets of rolls and an overall length of 50 feet, required even greater accuracy and a procedure capable of detecting errors of 2 thousandths of an inch was developed and applied.

Some requests for help came from other scientific laboratories. When the large radio telescope of the CSIRO Division of Radiophysics was installed at Parkes, in central New South Wales, it was necessary to measure with high accuracy any departures from the nominal shape of the dish under operating conditions. Puttock also undertook this task in 1963, developing

Part of the dimensional survey of the 64 m radio telescope at Parkes.

equipment with a discrimination of better than 1 millimetre at the edge of the dish. A semi-automatic system for rapid measurement of deformation of the surface was designed and installed in 1964.

The telescope was originally designed to receive radiation of wavelengths down to about 10 cm. Encouraging results from experiments at wavelengths down to 3.4 cm led to a decision in 1969 to replace wire mesh panels in the inner part of the dish with high-quality sheet metal panels in order to increase the reflectivity at shorter wavelengths. Puttock and Mr K. Loughry collaborated with the staff of the Division of Radiophysics in the installation and precise adjustment of the new surface plates. The modification allows the telescope to operate satisfactorily at wavelengths down to 1 cm.

The Laboratory has been called on to assist in dealing with problems in large-scale metrology on many later occasions. The demand has lessened in recent years as some surveyors now have the specialised equipment and techniques necessary, but continuing effort in relation to geodetic measurements is necessary. The introduction of electronic distance measuring instruments in the past twenty-five years has led to extensive changes in surveying practice in Australia and has brought new demands for calibration of instruments and baselines. The Laboratory has been closely involved in measurements associated with the revision of geodetic surveys of Australia. It was involved from the late 1940s in an Australian levelling survey which culminated in 1971 in the adoption of an Australian height datum.

In 1980, a 650 m geodetic base was installed in the grounds of the Laboratory. Together with the Laboratory's frequency standards, it allows the calibration of electronic distance measuring instruments with direct traceability to the national standards, providing both increased accuracy and much more rapid and convenient calibration than with earlier methods. The site of the base was chosen after consultation with the acknowledged world authority on baselines, Professor Kukkamaki, Director of the Finnish Geodetic Institute, and meets all the physical requirements for a satisfactory baseline. The calibration of an instrument requires the making of measurements over several known distances and the base has several measurement pillars.

Work is in progress to enable the distances between the pillars to be measured directly by multiple-wavelength laser interferometry based on a carbon-dioxide laser developed in the Laboratory.

Gear Measurement

Work on the measurement of gears began in the mid-1950s when gears were being made at the Ordnance Factory, Bendigo, for Australian-built ships. Later, the increasing use of large gears in mineral extraction and agricultural processing led to greater emphasis on measurement of such gears, which are often used in hostile conditions in locations remote from technical centres. Clearly, there was a need for *in situ* measurements and work was started on the development of equipment. This work has continued and has entered a new phase in the past few years. In 1983, a conference involving large-gear manufacturers and users was held at the Laboratory. This led to an agreement within the Applied Physics Industrial Program for collaboration in the further development of portable instruments. The manufacturers were A. Goninan and Company, Newcastle, New South Wales and the Ordnance Factory, Bendigo, Victoria, and the users were the Sugar Research Institute, Mackay, Queensland and Utah Development Co. Ltd., Brisbane, Queensland. The very large gears used in mineral processing and sugar milling, some up to 7 metres in diameter, are very expensive. It is necessary not only to be able to measure gears at the point of manufacture but also to measure them after use. This allows for planning of replacements and may make it possible to replace one of a pair of gears rather than both.

Portable axial pitch gear measuring instrument.

The research program, undertaken by a group headed by Mr E.G. Thwaite, has led to the development of a portable instrument for the measurement of the axial pitch of helical gears. A prototype instrument was constructed and tested in the measurement of some large gears in the plant of one of the sponsoring companies and two instruments have now been manufactured by the Tasmanian Development Authority. Some progress has also been made with the development of further instrumentation for the measurement of tooth form and other characteristics of gears.

Bridges for Resistance Thermometry

In the development of techniques for the measurement of temperature with platinum resistance thermometers, the need for better resistance-measuring instruments was recognised. In 1971, a high-precision ac bridge was described in a paper presented by Mr A.M. Thompson at the Fifth Symposium on "Temperature: Its Measurement in Science and Industry" in Washington, USA. The bridge is suitable for use in temperature measurement in standards laboratories, where the highest possible accuracy is required. It is capable of measurement to about 0.001 K over a range from about 50 K to over 700 K. It has been made commercially by J.J. Lloyd Instruments, Southampton, UK.

In 1971, Mr C.P. Pickup developed a low-cost ac bridge capable of reading directly to 0.01 ohm, which made it possible to measure temperature to a few hundredths of a degree. As no comparable instrument was commercially available, arrangements were made with Leeds and Northrup Australia Pty. Ltd. for manufacture under licence. More than 500 instruments have been sold in Australia and overseas.

A Precise Electronic Voltage Reference

Until recently, standards of electromotive force or voltage were usually maintained by means of standard cells. If cells are carefully maintained, they are capable of providing satisfactory voltage references but they are fragile and subject to damage in transport. In 1983, a collaborative project on the development of a portable electronic standard of comparable accuracy was started in the Laboratory within the Applied Physics Industrial Program. The work was undertaken by a group led by Mr I.K. Harvey in collaboration with the Sydney firm Statronics Power Supplies.

The Statronics VS4 Voltage Standard developed contains four independent reference units, each providing an output of 10 V and one of 1.018 V to allow immediate substitution for standard cells. It is based on carefully chosen and treated zener diodes. Drift rates are very low, being initially of the order of 3 parts per million per year, with progressive improvement through aging during use. Commercial production for both Australian and overseas markets has begun.

Monitoring Rail Wear

The transport of iron ore in Australia involves very long trains travelling at high speeds with some of the highest axle loadings in the world. Rail replacements are costly, but delay in replacing worn rails could lead to derailments. Although it has been possible for many of the characteristics of rails to be monitored from inspection vehicles moving at the same speed as load-carrying trains, until recently, rail head wear could be determined only by making spot checks at intervals along the tracks.

In 1977, Hamersley Iron Pty. Ltd. approached the Laboratory for assistance in developing instrumentation for non-contact measurement of the wear of rail heads from vehicles moving at 80 km per hour. Several possible systems

*A batch of Statronics portable DC voltage standards being delivered to the
Laboratory for calibration after manufacture.*

were discussed and one was fully developed by Mr G.W. Small and Mr Z.S.
Hegedus. It is capable of determining the profile of the rail head at intervals
of 5 m with an uncertainty of about 0.1 mm.

The unit is mounted under the inspection vehicle a short distance above the
rail. Light from a xenon flash tube is reflected by a pair of mirrors through
slit apertures on to either side of the rail head and web, so that a narrow line
of light follows the profile of the rail. This line is viewed by two cameras, each
of which forms an image on a solid-state image processor. The signals from
these are processed by computer to give the profile of the rail, which
is compared with stored information on the nominal profile. The
measurements are correlated with position along the track and, as well as
allowing optimisation of the rail replacement program, the system provides
information on wear rates and their relation to the track geometry. The
Perth firm Aldetec Pty. Ltd. has developed the equipment for commercial
production under licence, with the trade-name LITESLICE.

Applications of Ultrasonic Techniques

Research on the use of sound energy with frequencies above those audible to the human ear was started in the late 1970s. It has led to several applications in industry. When the problem of measuring rail wear described above was brought to the attention of the Laboratory, one possibility that was considered was the development of an ultrasonic device. Although this was not the approach finally chosen, research on the application of ultrasonics by Dr K. Hews-Taylor led to the development of equipment for precise non-contact distance measurement, especially where soft surfaces were involved. The instrument incorporated specially developed transducers capable of producing and detecting ultrasound in the frequency range from 50 to 200 kHz.

The production of this device led to a suggestion from the CSIRO Division of Environmental Mechanics that an ultrasonic instrument for the measurement of air velocity might be developed. Collaboration between the two Divisions and Dobbie Instruments (Australia) Pty. Ltd. led to the

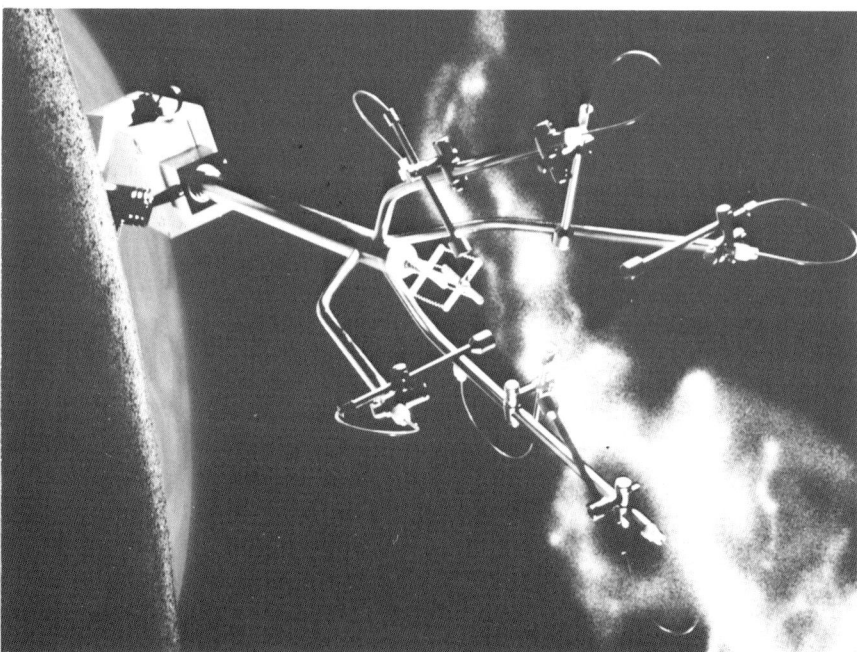

Smoke is used to detect air movement during the testing of an ultrasonic anemometer the Laboratory helped develop. The time difference between the propagation of ultrasound along forward and back paths in 3 orthogonal directions allows the true vector wind velocity to be calculated.

production at a competitive price of an anemometer with characteristics superior to those of other available instruments. It incorporates three pairs of transducers and is capable of measuring true vector wind velocity with high accuracy. It responds very quickly to changes in velocity and gives accurate measurements even at very low velocities.

Ultrasonic techniques are also being applied in the examination of steel castings for the detection of internal flaws. Research was undertaken within the Applied Physics Industrial Program by Dr D.C. Price in collaboration with the Steel Company of Australia Pty. Ltd. The project has involved research into complex ultrasonic scanning techniques, signal processing of ultrasound echoes, and image generation and processing. The device has been shown to be capable of detection and accurate measurement of defects in solids and further development is proceeding.

Dr Price has also developed equipment for measuring eccentricity of the bore of copper tubing during extrusion. This was an Applied Physics Industrial Program project in collaboration with Metal Manufactures Ltd., Port Kembla. As departures from concentricity of the bore and the exterior surface of tubing result in variations in wall thickness, it is important that eccentricity is reduced to a minimum. The equipment has three probes mounted around the tubing so that each transmits ultrasonic pulses at right angles to the axis of the tubing and records the echoes from the outer and inner surfaces. A microcomputer converts the time differences between the echo signals to a percentage eccentricity figure and also indicates the minimum wall thickness.

Water-Vapour and Humidity Measurements

Work in the field of water vapour and humidity measurement was started in the Laboratory in the 1940s. In 1945, the CSIR Division of Radiophysics needed in-flight humidity measurements in investigating the suspicion that the newly discovered phenomenon of "anomalous propagation" of radar might be caused by layering effects in the lower atmosphere. Dr R.G. Wylie developed a psychrometer that could operate in the slipstream of an aircraft and give readings on moving-coil meters, which were the only suitable indicating instruments then available. The same instrumentation was later used by the Division of Radiophysics in its rainmaking and cloud-physics investigations. A different psychrometer developed later by Wylie for use in a helicopter made it possible for the Division of National Mapping of the Department of National Development to achieve a significant increase in the accuracy of microwave distance measurements.

In 1957, Wylie developed a very precise automatic hygrometer which depends on the production, by uptake of water from air, of thin films of saturated solution on the surfaces of ionic single crystals. The thickness of the film is held constant by a servo system which controls the temperature of the air and the humidity can be derived from the temperature that is established. The instrument was made commercially in small numbers by Fairey Aviation Co. of A/asia Pty. Ltd. In one application, it was used by the US National Satellite Centre to obtain data on the infrared absorption of moist air as a function of humidity for the first Nimbus meteorological satellites. It was also used in investigations relating to the Swinbank eddy-flux method, developed in the CSIRO Division of Meteorological Physics, for determining the flux of water vapour in the lower atmosphere.

A differential psychrometer devised by Wylie in 1962 was used by the CSIRO Division of Land Research and Regional Survey in a study of the transpiration of plant leaves to measure small differences in the water-vapour content of two similar airstreams. The method was also used later by the CSIRO Division of Animal Genetics to study the transpiration of cattle.

Monitoring Conveyor Belts

In 1979, a request was received by the Laboratory for assistance in the examination of conveyor belts used for transporting coal. Failures of conveyor belts can result in extensive damage and substantial loss of production. The main problem with such belts is corrosion of the steel reinforcement cords and the method then in use for detection of corrosion was X-ray examination. This could only be applied to belts either stationary or moving very slowly and there were problems with protection of operators from exposure to X-rays.

Dr A. Harrison began an investigation of the possibility of using magnetic methods to detect changes in the characteristics of the reinforcing steel of belts while in use. His work led to the development of a conveyor belt monitor. Signals from sensors close to the belt surface vary with changes in magnetic reluctance. These signals are processed electronically to indicate changes in the mass of steel in the belt and the thickness of the cover of rubber. The instrument also indicates any breaks in the reinforcement. After initial collaboration with three firms, a Sydney firm, Conveyor Belt Monitoring, was exclusively licensed to use the technology. Recently, the marketing of the equipment has been taken over by a new company, Incor Ltd. In addition to extensive use in Australia, the technology is now in commercial use in Europe, the United States and more recently in Africa, Asia and the Pacific area. It is used not only for examination of operating belts but also for initial examination of newly manufactured belts.

Under a recent two-year agreement between the Laboratory and Incor,

Conveyor belt monitor being used to search for faults in a steel-cord conveyor belt operating in a West German underground coal mine. The non-destructive technique for scanning the conveyor belt was invented by Dr A. Harrison from the Laboratory and has international patents.

further applications of the technology are being evaluated. The monitor is being used to evaluate composite splices using signature analysis of the monitor signals and video graphic representation of the results. A new device using capacitance techniques has been developed to monitor belts with fabric reinforcement.

Vibration Measurement and Control

Problems arising from vibration were brought to the attention of the laboratory soon after its establishment. In dealing with the many requests for help in wartime production, it was often made aware of vibration problems. For the development of effective means of dealing with such problems, accurate measurement of the characteristics of the vibration is necessary, and capability in measurements of this kind was developed by a group led by Mr J.A. Macinante. Techniques for the mounting of vibration sources and of vibration-sensitive equipment so as to minimise the transmission of vibration were also developed.

Examination of 500 MW generator coils at the Liddell power station prior to vibration analysis.

By the late 1950s, instruments for the measurement of vibration over a wide range of frequencies and amplitudes had been developed and it was possible to assist with many industrial and laboratory problems. In 1957, a jig borer weighing about 20 tons was installed by Cockatoo Docks and Engineering Co. Pty. Ltd. On the advice of the Laboratory, it was mounted on a concrete block weighing about 30 tons supported by sixteen coil springs, with frictional dampers. Vibration transmission was reduced to a satisfactory level. At about the same time, a large roll-grinding machine at Austral Bronze Co. Pty. Ltd., Sydney, was successfully mounted on a similar "seismic" block supported on rubber isolators. The total weight of the machine, the block and the rolls being ground was about 115 tons.

The techniques developed for the use of seismic mountings were described in the book "Seismic mountings for vibration isolation", by J.A. Macinante, published by Wiley Interscience in 1984.

Vibration investigations have continued and a significant example of their value was an investigation of the causes of failure of several large generators in a New South Wales power station. Four identical 500 MW generators were commissioned between 1971 and 1973. Three of them failed within a short period in 1981. Investigation by a team led by Dr J.L. Goldberg showed that vibration induced by magnetic forces had led to the failure of flexible connectors at the ends of the stator windings. Analysis of the vibration patterns made it possible to establish the existence of faulty conductors in the fourth generator, which had not failed, and to determine their positions. Subsequently, the fault condition was verified after partial dismantling and removal of insulation.

In another recent investigation in collaboration with the State Rail Authority of New South Wales, Goldberg has studied the radiation of noise from plate-web girder bridges when trains pass over them. Analysis of measurements made on a bridge over the new F-3 freeway at the northern Sydney suburb Wahroonga showed a significant correlation between the frequencies of the radiated noise and those of structural vibration. Vibration of the plate webs leads to the emission of noise in the frequency range of 40 to 90 Hz, which is propagated over considerable distances. The modes of vibration and their interactions are now well understood and it appears that it may be possible to reduce the noise propagation significantly through the use of tuned-mass dampers on the plate webs. Information derived from the analysis has provided the guidance necessary for positioning these dampers and further work is being undertaken to evaluate the reduction that can be achieved by this method.

Electrical Measurements at Power Frequencies

Instruments for measuring ac electric current, voltage and power must be calibrated in terms of the basic electrical units by the use of ac-to-dc transfer standards. The Laboratory has collaborated with the Sydney County Council over many years in the development of special-purpose instruments for use in calibration. One is a transportable ac-dc thermal power transfer standard. This instrument is being further developed as a travelling standard for use by NATA-registered laboratories. A protection circuit has been developed for a commercial ac-dc thermal voltage and current transfer instrument used as a travelling standard in the Asia/Pacific Metrology Programme.

Electrical quantities in industry are often too large to be measured directly. Where such measurements are needed, transformers are used to derive currents or voltages that can be measured conveniently and that are known accurately in terms of the original currents or voltages. The instrument transformers used must be calibrated and periodically re-calibrated. The Laboratory some years ago, again in collaboration with the Sydney County Council, developed special equipment to expedite instrument transformer testing. A current transformer with adjustable errors has also been developed and used in proficiency testing of NATA laboratories.

Recent improvements in technology have led to the availability of sophisticated digital instruments capable of high accuracy and stability. A new reference standard calibration system has been established in the Laboratory to provide, in conjunction with NATA, a service to industry in Australia. The system provides both ac and dc voltage calibrations in terms of the national ac-dc transfer standards and is capable of calibrating the most accurate digital instruments currently available or likely to become available in the near future.

In the past two years, under the Applied Physics Industrial Program, a precision power amplifier has been developed, in collaboration with University Paton Instruments, by Mr J.R. Fiander in a group led by Dr B.D. Inglis. This is a very stable instrument that can be used for a wide range of laboratory and industry calibrations. It operates from dc up to 100 kHz with output voltages up to 1200 V at powers up to 1500 W.

Radio-Frequency and Microwave Measurements

Along with the development of capability to meet a continuing demand for new types of calibrations in the radio-frequency and microwave range, the Laboratory has developed some special-purpose instruments for use at microwave frequencies. With increasing domestic and commercial use of microwave ovens in the early 1970s, the need for a simple device for detecting leakage of microwave energy was recognised. A simple, inexpensive and reliable instrument was developed by a group led by Dr D.L. Hollway. It does not rely on batteries or other power supplies but is designed to be activated by the microwave energy in a stray field. The tester has been manufactured under licence for some years by Electrosafe Pty. Ltd., of Melbourne, and over 100 000 units have been sold.

The group, led more recently by Mr P.I. Somlo, has also developed a microwave moisture monitor. It functions by reacting to changes in the absorption of microwave energy and has been shown to be effective for measuring moisture levels in materials as diverse as raw sugar, timber and glass-reinforced synthetic resin. It can also be used for locating anomalies in solid structures such as timber studs behind plaster walls.

High-Voltage Research

Research relating to the transmission of electrical energy at high voltages was limited by the space and facilities available in the original laboratory for work of this kind. Even so, there was a substantial program of testing and research and several devices developed in the Laboratory, especially in connection with electric power transmission, were produced commercially. The availability of a much more satisfactory high-voltage laboratory and of

106

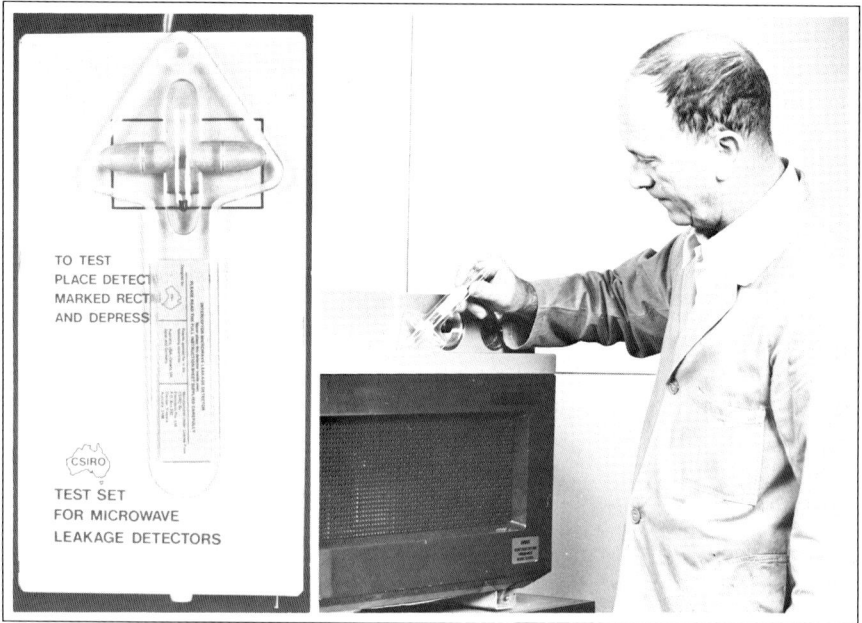

The Laboratory's microwave leak detector – (left) testing to see it performs to specification; (right) checking a microwave oven for radiation leakage.

suitable outdoor space at the Lindfield site made it possible to undertake experimental work on power transmission problems that had not previously been feasible. The high-voltage laboratory is operated in collaboration with the Electricity Commission of New South Wales and, in addition to its basic use for calibrations and measurements, has been used in studies essential for the design of 500 kV transmission lines now being installed. A mobile calibration unit can transport equipment for calibrations in other laboratories.

Knowledge of the temperatures likely to be reached in the conductors is very important in the design of transmission lines. In 1982, a major study on the thermal behaviour of overhead high-voltage lines was initiated by Dr V.T. Morgan, in conjunction with the Electricity Commission of New South Wales, with the aim of applying probabilistic methods to the rating of lines. This involved the construction of an experimental outdoor transmission line with appropriate instrumentation. Observations were made over several years and the effects of changes in the sixteen variables influencing the temperatures are being evaluated. The work has confirmed some features of design information obtained from wind-tunnel studies but has also revealed important differences. Some of the results of the work are discussed in a book "The Thermal Behaviour of Electric Conductors" by Dr Morgan, to be published during 1988 by Research Studies Press, New York.

Superconductivity

Following the construction of the Laboratory's first helium liquefier in 1950, a significant background of experience in low-temperature physics was built up in the Laboratory. Research with superconducting devices began in 1969, when the development of a voltage standard based on the Josephson effect was started by Mr I.K. Harvey. By 1970, a standard of this kind was operational and has continued in service since then. With this introduction to the field of superconductivity, Harvey initiated work on applications of superconductivity in a range of new devices operating at liquid helium temperatures. The work was concerned initially with precision electrical measurements but has been extended into other fields.

In 1987, work began on high-temperature superconductivity following the discovery overseas of new materials that become superconducting at temperatures above the boiling point of nitrogen, 77 K. The considerable breadth of expertise available in the Laboratory was dedicated to the manufacture and characterisation of the new materials and the first break-junction SQUIDS made from one of these materials were produced.

A project led by Dr J.C. Macfarlane has been set up to continue investigations on the properties and potential of the new materials. In these investigations, scientists in the Laboratory are collaborating with Amalgamated Wireless (A/asia) Ltd., the Broken Hill Proprietary Co. Ltd. and Ausonics Pty. Ltd. Recently, the Federal Department of Industry, Technology and Commerce has made a grant of $380 000 for this work under the Grants for Industrial Research and Development (GIRD) scheme, and additional funding has also been provided by the firms concerned.

In research relating to another application of superconductivity, Dr G.J. Sloggett is collaborating with medical research workers at Westmead Hospital in the development and use of highly sensitive detectors of magnetic activity of the brain. The detectors are SQUIDS (see page 64), which are sufficiently sensitive to allow the location of the small neural electric currents that are the sources of magnetic activity within the brain. The mapping of the magnetic fields and the localisation of the sources require sophisticated computer processing of the signals from the detectors. These investigations are providing information essential for the development of diagnostic techniques based on direct imaging of brain electrical activity to supplement information obtained by existing techniques such as magnetic resonance imaging.

Satellite Time Dissemination

Time and frequency standards in the Laboratory are maintained by two commercially made caesium beam clocks and two hydrogen masers designed and constructed in the Laboratory. The Laboratory is linked to the major timing laboratories of the world and to some other laboratories in Australia by the Global Positioning System (GPS) navigational satellites. This ensures that Australia's time standards are linked to international Coordinated Universal Time (UTC) to within 30 nanoseconds.

A new system of time dissemination in Australia is currently being developed. It will give remote users access to the time standards of the Laboratory through Australian Broadcasting Corporation (ABC) television transmissions from AUSSAT. A timing reference associated with the television transmission will be compared with the NML clock. Appropriate correction signals will be transferred to the ABC and incorporated into the television transmission. A microprocessor-based receiver will allow a user in a remote location, on entering the local latitude and longitude, to view a display giving the time to within 10 microseconds of the Australian standard. Arrangements for commercial production of receivers are being discussed.

Holography

In 1963, Dr J.V. Ramsay constructed in the Laboratory the first gas laser to operate in Australia, and in 1964, a helium-neon laser based on his design was produced commercially by the Adelaide firm Scientific Optical Laboratories of Australia. Shortly afterwards, Dr W.H. Steel and Mr R.N. Smartt used a helium-neon laser to record a hologram, which is a record of an object in the form of an interference pattern that can be reconstructed by suitable illumination to give a three-dimensional image of the original object. Work in the development of holography has continued. In 1971, the possibility of using holographic methods to detect defects in motor car tyres was investigated by Dr J.L. Goldberg.

In 1973, Dr P. Hariharan developed improved processing methods which gave high-quality reflection holograms. The reconstruction of holograms to give images of the original subjects normally requires illumination with monochromatic light, but in 1977, Hariharan devised techniques for producing holograms that could give bright, multi-colour images when illuminated with white light.

Work on the application of holographic interferometry has continued and in 1985, led to the development of a computer-based system allowing the mapping in a few seconds of the deformation of a surface of an object

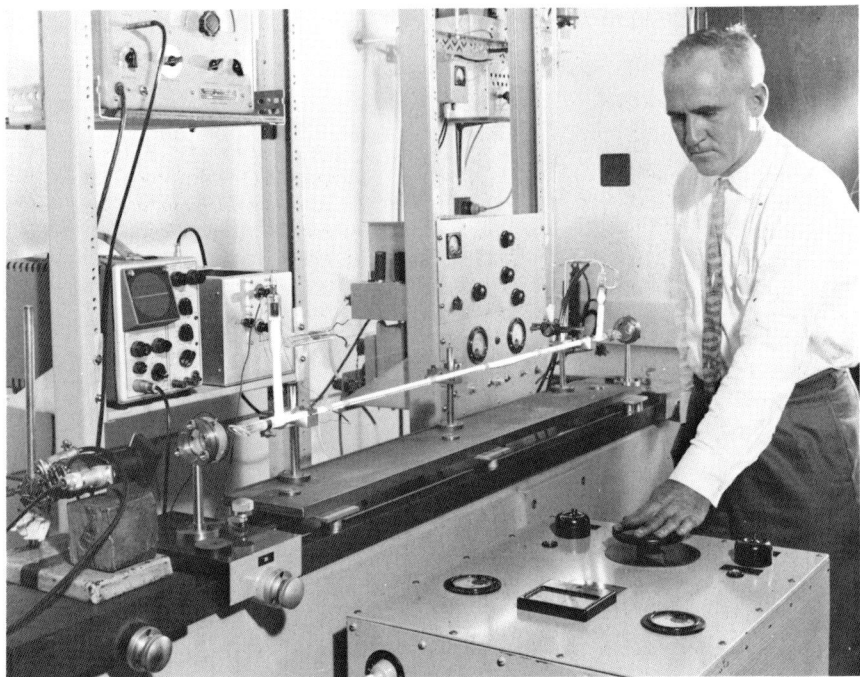

Dr J.V. Ramsay operating the first gas laser constructed in Australia.
Photo: May 1963.

subjected to stress, with an accuracy of about 3 nm. The system has been further developed with stroboscopic illumination to make measurements on vibrating objects.

Thin Films

In the deposition of thin films with particular properties on glass and other materials, it is usually desirable that the film should be uniform over a considerable area. A novel technique for controlling deposition was developed in 1974 by a group led by Dr J.V. Ramsay. An off-axis rotating shutter was introduced into the vacuum chamber between the source and the surface to be treated. With appropriate positioning of the shutter and shaping of its profile, very uniform thin films could be deposited. Shutter profiles were also developed to allow controlled deposition for correction of non-uniformity. An example was the deposition of glass on the plates of the triple Fabry-Perot interferometer described on page 86. Errors of flatness on plates of 54 mm diameter were reduced to less than 1 nm, allowing a substantial improvement in the performance of the interferometer.

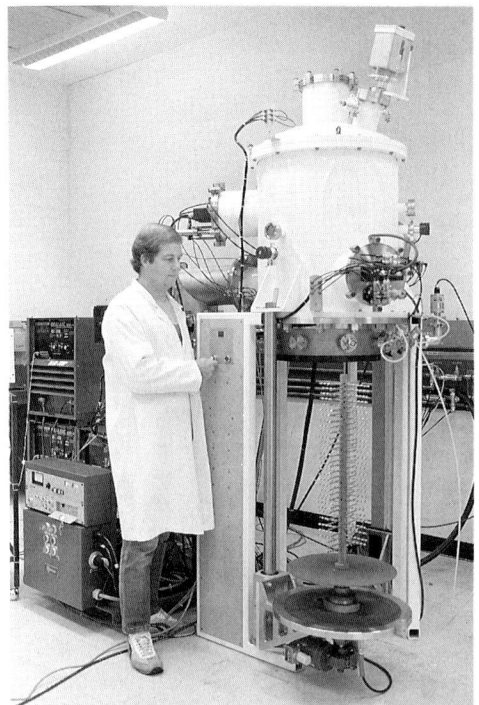

Pilot plant for the titanium nitride coating of cutting tools. Drills on a conveyor line (bottom right) are drawn into the deposition chamber where a 3-gun arc-deposition system is employed for the coating process.

A problem with some vacuum-deposited thin films has been instability of the films. This instability has been associated with the formation in the films of columnar structures separated by voids, which can form fine capillaries, allowing the entry of water vapour. In 1982, Dr R.P. Netterfield and Dr P.J. Martin showed that films with superior characteristics can be produced by irradiating the films with low-energy charged particles during deposition. This has the effect of increasing the mobility of the atoms being deposited, so that any microvoids and capillaries are sealed.

A similar technique has been applied in the production of wear-resistant coatings on metal-cutting tools. Ion-assisted deposition of titanium nitride has led to tool life being increased by as much as tenfold. In a collaborative program with Sutton Tools Pty. Ltd. and Surface Technology, improved coating equipment is being developed and the causes of tool failure are being investigated.

Ion-Molecule Reactions

In 1971, a small group led by Dr K.R. Ryan transferred to the Laboratory from the Upper Atmosphere Section of CSIRO. The group had been concerned with reactions between ions and molecules in the upper

111

atmosphere and it was arranged that this work would be continued and extended as part of the program of the Laboratory. From about 1974, attention was given to the reactions leading to the development of ozone from motor vehicle exhaust products in the lower atmosphere. For this work, a gas-flow reactor was constructed and the species resulting from the reactions were identified and measured in a mass spectrometer. It was shown that organic peroxy radicals reacted rapidly with nitric oxide to produce nitrogen dioxide, which in turn led to the production of ozone.

In the last few years, the research work has been largely on the somewhat similar reactions that are involved in semiconductor etching processes and plasma processes for surface coating. Such studies are essential for the development of new technologies in the related industries. The reactions involved in etching with fluorine compounds in oxygen plasmas are now well understood and attention is being given to plasma processes for the deposition of materials such as silicon and diamond.

Gaseous Electronics

Although electric arc welding has been used for many years, precise knowledge of the phenomena in the column of plasma between the electrodes has been scanty. A group led by Dr G.N. Haddad has been collaborating with the Australian Welding Research Association in a program to develop better understanding of these phenomena. The work has provided information allowing a more rational approach to the design of welding processes, particularly those for automated welding.

The group has also investigated the possibilities of plasma smelting of minerals in collaboration with the CSIRO Division of Mineral Chemistry and with the Broken Hill Proprietary Co. Ltd. One aspect studied has been the interaction of plasma arcs with magnetic fields. A 120 kW pilot plasma reactor has been constructed at the Melbourne laboratory of the Division of Mineral Chemistry and used, among other things, in experiments on the dissociation of zircon sands. Some work on applications of plasma spraying for the production of protective or decorative coatings has also been undertaken in collaboration with interested firms.

Viscosity Measurement

Since 1969, the Laboratory has made available samples of liquids of certified viscosity for use in calibrating viscometers. The service was initiated by Dr R.G. Wylie and is based on work in the Laboratory over many years on the development of a reliable viscosity scale. Liquids of six types are available. They range in nominal kinematic viscosity from 2.5 to 600 mm^2/s (centistokes) at 25 and 40°C. About 150 samples are issued per year.

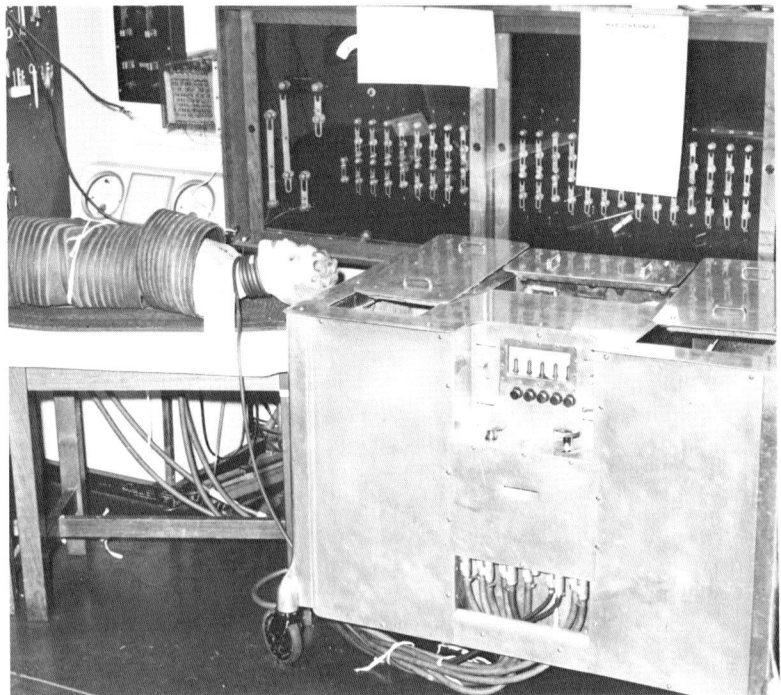

Demonstration of "cold blanket" equipment developed to cool adult patients prior to surgery.

Medical Science

In 1954, Mr A.F.A. Harper and Dr R.G. Wylie collaborated with Dr M.H. Cass in the development of equipment for controlled hypothermia. This involved cooling the patient bodily to approximately 28°C before and during surgery. At this temperature, it was possible to interrupt the blood flow safely for a period long enough for surgery such as operations to the heart. Up to that time, hypothermia had been applied in Australia only to infants, who were cooled in baths of ice. The poor control of temperature with this method would have involved unacceptable risks with adults.

Harper and Wylie developed "cold blanket" equipment to cool and rewarm adult patients, and direct-reading instruments for measuring the patient's internal temperature. The rubber blankets, made from drawings prepared in the Laboratory, were donated by Dunlop Rubber Australia Ltd., and Ebsray Pumps Pty. Ltd. lent suitable pumps and other facilities. After the performance of the apparatus was proved in surgical operations on sheep, Harper and Wylie collaborated with Dr Cass in its first application in operations on human patients. Dr Cass was later a Member of the House of Representatives and became Minister for the Environment and Conservation in 1973 and Minister for the Media in 1975.

From 1947, the Laboratory, in collaboration with the New South Wales Red Cross Blood Bank, maintained a standard scale for the estimation of haemoglobin in blood on the basis of measurement of the optical absorption of the derivative oxyhaemoglobin. In 1963, Dr W.R. Blevin, in collaboration with Dr I.D.P. Wootton, of the Postgraduate Medical School, London, investigated the use of cyanmethaemoglobin as a more stable derivative. They showed that the then accepted value for the optical density was too high and in August 1963, the European Society of Haematology recommended the adoption of a lower value. Later, the International Committee for Standardization in Haematology established an international haemoglobin scale based in part on Dr Blevin's measurements.

The thin slices of biological material that are required for microscopic examination are cut with microtomes, and the microtome knives must be sharpened frequently. The difficulties of ensuring adequate sharpness were brought to the attention of the Laboratory by Sydney pathologists in 1957. The technique of lapping had been used extensively in the Laboratory for surface finishing of metals. Mr G.A. Bell investigated the possibility of producing fine cutting edges by using this technique, in which metal surfaces are worked on a plate of relatively soft metal with abrasive material embedded in it. He devised the necessary equipment, which included an adjustable holder to maintain a knife at the correct angle to the lapping plate during the process. With this equipment, edges superior to those obtainable with the conventional honing process could be produced in about a tenth of the time. The equipment has been produced commercially in Australia and the United Kingdom with the trade name SI-RO-KEEN.

In a recent project under the Applied Physics Industrial Program, Dr J.C. Macfarlane and Dr G. Harding have collaborated with Cochlear Pty. Ltd. in investigating the possibility of using thin-film techniques in the production of cochlear implants. These are parts of equipment developed in the University of Melbourne to give partial hearing to profoundly deaf people. The Division has also provided technical advice that has been used in obtaining approval by medical authorities in the United States for the existing multi-wire implant.

The expertise developed in the Laboratory in spectroradiometry has led to many contacts with medical research workers interested in the properties of ultraviolet radiation. It has been known for many years that the biological effects differ in different parts of the ultraviolet spectrum. Recent collaboration between Mr F.J. Wilkinson and medical and veterinary scientists has led to more precise knowledge of the biological effects of radiation of various wavelengths and to the development of a new phototherapy appliance.

Investigations in collaboration with Professor C.H. Gallagher, of the Department of Veterinary Pathology, University of Sydney, are providing information on the production of carcinomas on the skins of animals and on the effects of both photosensitising and screening agents. In another project, in collaboration with Professor P. Hersey, of the Department of Oncology and Immunology of the Royal Newcastle Hospital, the effects of the ultraviolet content of natural and artificial sunlight on human immune system responses are being studied. Prototype lamps designed for producing ultraviolet radiation with spectral characteristics appropriate for human and animal wound-healing applications have been tested by research workers at the Prince of Wales Hospital, the Skin and Cancer Foundation at St Vincent's Hospital, Sydney, and equine veterinary practices in Queensland and Victoria. The lamps incorporate a specially designed multi-layer filter developed in the Laboratory to limit transmission to the wavelengths that sterilise infected surface tissues and promote wound healing.

In conventional radio transmission, the signals are carried by electromagnetic waves. In the vicinity of a transmitter, there is also an induction field, and this is utilised in a communication system devised by Mr V.R. Burgess during the 1970s. The system has been developed initially to enable people with impaired hearing to receive amplified speech without amplification of background noise. In particular, it can help children with impaired hearing to learn language and to take part in conversation. The system has a range of about 12 m and, when used in a school class, allows a student to hear the teacher's voice through a hearing aid without amplification of unwanted sounds. Because the induction field is localised, problems of interference that would be inevitable with normal radio transmission are avoided.

Following testing of the system in collaboration with the National Acoustics Laboratory of the Department of Health, tenders were called for the development of equipment for commercial production. The tender of Plessey Australia Pty. Ltd. was accepted and transmitter and receiver units produced by Plessey are in use in many schools.

The system has potential for other applications. It can be used by children in the home as well as in school and also can help adults with impaired hearing. It is being installed in the new Parliament House in Canberra so that visitors will be able to hear the debates and the voices of guides clearly. The

Induction-field wireless hearing aid being used in a remedial class at St Gabriels.

possibility of installation in concert halls and other public buildings is also being investigated.

Courses and Seminars

Soon after the war, it was realised that there was a need for improvement in the level of expertise in temperature measurement in industry and in many scientific laboratories. As there was no formal course available, a school was arranged. Those taking part spent several days in the Laboratory and were involved in practical work as well as lectures. The success of the school led to demands for repetition and similar schools have been held at intervals since.

As scientific and industrial procedures involving very low temperatures became more widely used, a need for training in low-temperature techniques was recognised. In 1973, a one-week course in cryogenic technology was conducted in the Laboratory and similar courses have been arranged more recently. In 1974, a course in Precise Electrical Measurement was conducted. With the improved facilities at the Lindfield

116

site, it has become possible for such courses to be arranged much more conveniently and efficiently. In addition to courses extending over several days, one-day seminars on specialised fields of measurement have been held.

Artists in Residence

In 1982, the Australia Council approached CSIRO suggesting closer liaison between the organisations in view of the increasing importance of new technology in relation to art. After preliminary discussion, it was decided that a pilot program should be arranged in the Laboratory. Proposals from artists were invited in advertisements in 1983 and those received were assessed in collaboration with the Australia Council and the Australian Film Commission.

Four fellowships were awarded. Moya Henderson, a Sydney musician, had invented a new keyboard instrument, the alemba, which incorporated metal triangles with tubular resonators. She worked in collaboration with Dr D.L.H. Gibbings and other scientists concerned with acoustics to improve the performance and tuning of the instrument. Alexander, a Sydney sculptor and holographic artist, worked with Dr P. Hariharan and other scientists in the Laboratory to produce large white-light holograms that have since been exhibited in the Pompidou Centre in Paris, the Sao Paulo Biennial, the Australian Pavilion in Expo 85 in Japan, and in a one-man exhibition by Alexander in Sydney. Simon Biggs, an Adelaide computer artist, used computer-aided design equipment to produce computer graphics and to investigate the use of computer-based sensing in interactive environmental sculpture. Michael Scullion, an Adelaide film maker, also used the computer-aided design equipment to produce three-dimensional images which were filmed from the computer screen.

The program was reviewed by the Australia Council and the Division in 1984 and further residencies were advertised. Up to the end of 1987, there were altogether thirteen residencies, one being arranged jointly with the CSIRO Division of Geomechanics. In two cases, the residencies were taken up in the Melbourne Branch of the Division of Applied Physics. Further collaboration between artists and scientists, not only in the Laboratory but also in other scientific institutions, is being planned by the Australia Council through its Artists and New Technology Program.

The National Standards Laboratory, Sydney University grounds, Chippendale, Sydney. Photo: 20/5/1955

Aerial view of the National Standards Laboratory showing construction of the Chemistry School at Sydney University. Photo: 2/12/1957

Accommodation and Facilities

When the University of Sydney agreed in September 1938 to make a site in the grounds of the University available for the National Standards Laboratory, it specified that the design, plans and materials of the building were to be approved by the University. It was pointed out that "as the building will be aligned on the main building, the old Medical School, and the proposed new School of Chemistry, it will have to conform with these buildings, which will mean *inter alia*, that it will have to be built or faced with stone".

When the Executive Committee of CSIR was informed that the stone facing for the building would increase its cost by up to £8000, it asked the University Senate to reconsider the matter. The Senate insisted on this condition but the impasse was resolved when, after a hint that CSIR might consider locating the laboratory elsewhere, the Premier of New South Wales, Mr B.S.B. Stevens, wrote to the Prime Minister on 16 March 1939. The Premier indicated that he had been advised of the problem and wrote "The vital importance of the establishment of the National Standards Laboratory is fully appreciated by my Government, and in a desire to co-operate with the Commonwealth Government in this regard, I wish to inform you that the New South Wales Government is prepared to provide the necessary funds, not exceeding the estimated cost of £8,000, to enable a stone facing to be placed on the building with the object of keeping it in conformity with the existing University buildings, with which it will be associated".

The University authorities drew the attention of those concerned with the design of the building to the fact that the new Chemistry School of the University was also being planned. They recommended consultation with the University's architects so that the two buildings might be architecturally compatible. The buildings that were finally constructed were certainly not similar in architectural style. The NSL building, now known as the Madsen Building, was designed, as required by the University, to conform to the then existing University buildings. The Chemistry School, which was not built until several years later, after the end of the war, and other adjacent University buildings erected more recently, are typical examples of mid-century "glass-house" architecture.

The NSL building was designed largely on the basis of information made available from the United Kingdom National Physical Laboratory. In April 1939, the Minister gave his approval for the sketch plans to be sent to the

Commonwealth Department of Works for the preparation of detailed drawings. The cost was estimated at £60 000 without the stone facing required by the University. Tenders were let late in 1939.

Although the building had been approved and designed specifically for the National Standards Laboratory, wartime developments resulted in the first occupants being members of the staff of the newly formed Radiophysics Laboratory of CSIR. They began work in the first part of the building to be completed in March 1940. Members of the staff of the National Standards Laboratory began to move into other parts of the building later in 1940. The headquarters of the Radiophysics Laboratory, which later became the Division of Radiophysics, remained in the NSL building until 1968, when the Division moved to new accommodation in the northern Sydney suburb of Epping.

By 1944, the activities of the Laboratory had expanded to such an extent that additional accommodation was needed and approval for the completion of the building was given. Construction started in the middle of 1945, and was not completed until late in 1948. During the construction period, there was considerable disruption of the work of the Laboratory and extensive re-location of equipment and activities followed completion of the building.

The Committee on the National Standards Laboratory, set up in 1957 by the CSIR Advisory Council to "consider the present and future activities of the National Standards Laboratory", pointed out in its report that the accommodation of the Laboratory was grossly overcrowded. It recognised that the Division of Radiophysics would eventually vacate the part of the building it occupied but considered that the additional space that would be made available would be "completely inadequate to provide for the developments that should take place during the next few years".

To provide some temporary relief, an arrangement was made in 1959 for the lease of space in Alpha house, a building a short distance from the Laboratory, for use by the Applied Mechanics group of the Division of Metrology. Shortly afterwards, more space in the building was leased for work in relation to radio-frequency and microwave measurements and calibrations. The building had been used as a textile mill and was far from ideal for the purposes of the Laboratory.

The University of Sydney also by this time had an accommodation problem and indicated that it would prefer the Laboratory to be re-located so that the building could be used by the University. The Executive of the CSIRO recognised the need for new accommodation for the Laboratory and, with the cooperation of the Commonwealth Department of the Interior, a search for a suitable site was made. The aim was to find a site large enough to provide for foreseeable development, reasonably close to Sydney, with low levels of vibration and electrical interference.

The Lindfield Site

The land at Lindfield eventually selected already had an interesting history. In 1938, about 10 000 Boy Scouts from around the world attended a Jamboree on the site. It was then in relatively undisturbed bushland but a new road, Lady Game Drive, named after the wife of the Governor of the State, had been constructed near the site shortly before as a project to provide work for unemployed men during the depression of the 1930s.

During World War 2, the Royal Australian Air Force established an Initial Training School on the site. The buildings were later used for emergency housing, and part of the area was used for a migrant hostel until 1971. By the 1970s there was extensive suburban housing development adjacent to the site. Before the proposal for its use for the Laboratory was accepted, several proposals for other uses were rejected by the Council of the Municipality of Ku-ring-gai, in which it was located, as inappropriate for a residential area.

The site, of almost 30 ha, is about 12 km north-west from Sydney. The levels of vibration caused by traffic are low and should remain so as no roads for heavy traffic are likely to be constructed in the vicinity. There are strong television signals from transmitters about 3 km away but it was considered that acceptably low levels could be achieved within the Laboratory by suitable screening.

Design Considerations

Much valuable information relating to the design of the building was available from experience in metrology laboratories in other countries. While the site vibration levels were low, it was also necessary that the buildings should be designed so as to minimise the transmission of vibration resulting from essential activities in the laboratories and associated buildings. It was known from overseas experience that steel-framed and reinforced concrete buildings transmitted vibrations readily. It was also recognised that steel framing and reinforcement could lead to problems of electromagnetic interference. The main laboratories were therefore designed to be built with load-bearing brick walls, with only one floor above the ground floor, in three blocks separated by courtyards about 30 m wide, but linked by enclosed walkways. Two underground laboratory areas were provided for activities requiring long lines of sight.

Another major requirement was adequate control of environmental conditions in the laboratories. In order to provide for control of

Top: Bradfield Park site during the Boy Scouts Jamboree in 1938. Bottom: Aerial photo of the same site during the initial stages of construction of the National Measurement Laboratory. Bradfield Road has been re-routed to give a curved right angle bend to skirt the Laboratory site. The original road is still partly visible.

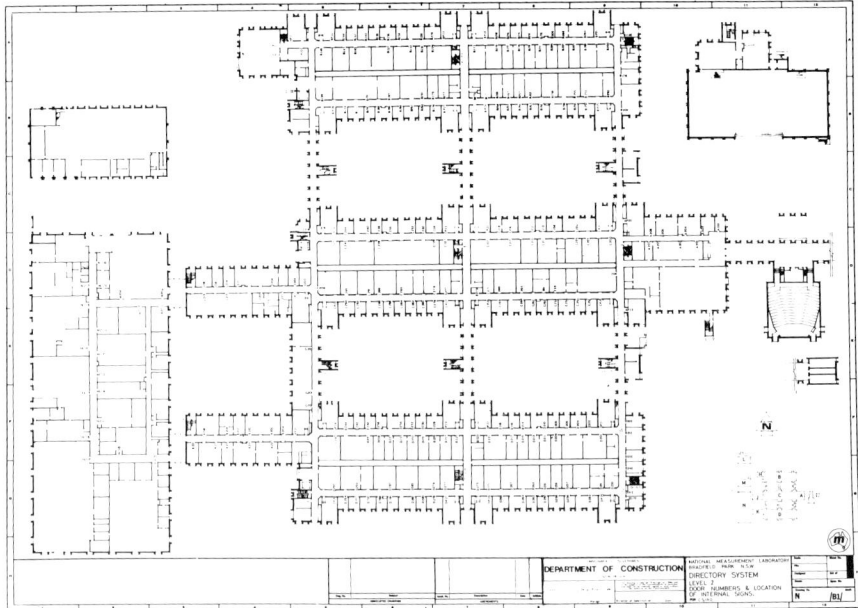

Lower floor plan of the National Measurement Laboratory.

temperatures within individual laboratory rooms within ±0.5°C in the range from 18°C to 23°C, and for relative humidity to be controlled to between 45% and 55%, the main laboratories were planned to be located in the central parts of each of the three blocks, with offices and less critical laboratories along the outer walls. With normal comfort air conditioning, these would protect the laboratories from variations in the outside environment and reduce the problems of meeting the temperature and humidity specifications for the laboratories themselves. Each laboratory block was designed with two rows of laboratory rooms separated by service ducts running the full length of the building and extending through the full height. Wet and gaseous services were arranged to be brought from these ducts through the back walls of the laboratories. A plan of one floor is shown above.

Because of the size of the project and lack of relevant experience in Australia, a full-scale model laboratory was built by engineers of the Department of Housing and Construction, and experiments were conducted to find the most satisfactory and economical way of achieving the conditions required. It was found that, if recirculating air was fed in a fan shape towards the walls from sides of a duct along the centre of the ceiling, good uniformity could be obtained. The rate of air circulation was about seven times as great as in normal comfort conditioning and air velocities were close to the maximum that could be tolerated by people working in the laboratories. More detailed information on the design of the Laboratory has been given in papers by M.R. Brown[1] and M.J. Puttock[2].

Transfer to Lindfield

The financial position of the CSIRO in the 1960s was such that it was suggested that it might be necessary to move the Laboratory to the new site in stages, possibly extending over several years. This would have led to very serious operating problems. The Department of Works strongly advised that the nature of the project made it highly desirable for the construction to be undertaken as a single operation. This advice was accepted by the CSIRO executive and construction was started in 1973. The move from the Sydney University site to Lindfield started early in 1977 and was completed by mid-1978.

The Laboratory as finally constructed included the three main laboratory blocks, a separate services building containing workshops and stores, a plant building some distance from the laboratories to provide hot and chilled water for the air-conditioning system and other services, an administrative building containing offices, a lecture theatre (named in 1987 the Lehany Theatre in honour of Mr F.J. Lehany) and a cafeteria, and a high-voltage laboratory separated from the other buildings. Each laboratory block is approximately 100 m long and 30 m wide. The floor space available is approximately double that of the old site.

The Laboratory was the last major Commonwealth building complex designed in the Imperial system of units. The laboratories are built on a 12 ft module, which is approximately 3.7 m. The corridors have a minimum clear width of 2 m to facilitate the movement of large pieces of equipment. In addition, the doors and windows of the offices are aligned with the doors of the laboratories to allow for the movement of equipment too long to be moved through the corridors. The floors of the ground-floor laboratories are concrete slabs 300 mm thick isolated from the structural walls to minimise vibration transmission problems.

The hot and chilled water for the air-conditioning system is supplied from the main plant room through tunnels to 55 air-handling plants distributed around the buildings. The arrangement of air ducts adopted give very satisfactory uniformity of temperature through a large proportion of the volume of each laboratory, with acceptable air velocities. The make-up air is saturated at a temperature such that, when it is mixed with the recirculating air at the correct temperature, the relative humidity is with the acceptable range.

Interior of the high-voltage laboratory with the bushing of the 600 kV trans-
former in the foreground and the 1.3 MV impulse generator in the background.
The monorail track on the ceiling accommodates the two hoists used for moving
equipment.

To minimise electrical interference from outside sources, especially from
television signals, the main laboratories have metal roofing and 13-mm wire
mesh, galvanised and plastic coated, in the wall cavities. The windows are
double-glazed with the inner surfaces of the outer panes metallised.

Considerable problems with air flow control required the replacement of
some mechanical parts after occupation of the buildings and there were also
difficulties with the electronic control systems. These were eventually
resolved by NML staff engineers, and experience with the system led to
some changes in both equipment and operating procedures, with the
eventual reduction of about one third in the operating cost.

The high-voltage laboratory was designed for ac voltages up to 1.2 MV and
impulse voltages up to 3.2 MV. It contains a large high-voltage hall, smaller
laboratories and offices, and there is an outside test area 30 m square. It is
the largest laboratory of its kind in Australia though far from the largest in

the world. The high-voltage hall is approximately 45 m long, 21 m wide and 19 m high, so that it can accommodate large pieces of equipment with adequate clearance between any equipment in use and the walls. The walls are lined with perforated steel plates backed by glass wool to reduce noise problems and there is an earth mat, connected to the wall lining, under the concrete floor and extending under and beyond the outside test area, with earthing points for equipment in a grid pattern. A door 15 m square provides for the movement into the high-voltage hall of large pieces of equipment and high voltages to be taken from the hall to the outside test area. Equipment within the hall can be moved by means of two monorail hoists with capacities of 10 t and 5 t.

The two major pieces of equipment are a 600 kV transformer and a 1.3 MV impulse generator. The transformer was moved from the Sydney University site, where it had been installed in 1963. The impulse generator is the property of the Electricity Commission of New South Wales, which operates the facility jointly with the Laboratory.

The 600 kV transformer being transferred from Sydney University to Lindfield.

Model of the 550 kN force machine

Force Calibration Machines

At the Sydney University site, it had not been possible to install a large force-calibrating machine, and standards for calibrating materials-testing machines had to be sent overseas for calibration. Special provision for accommodating a suitable machine was made when the Lindfield buildings were being designed. The machine was made by Avery in the United Kingdom and was delivered in 1973. It was therefore necessary for it to be stored for several years before it was possible to install it at Lindfield.

Forces exerted by gravity on known masses are used for calibrating load cells, proving rings and other force measuring devices. The masses can be loaded in small increments to give forces up to a maximum of 550 kN. The machine is about 9 m high and occupies an area of about 7 m². To allow for convenient operation and also to avoid raising the roof line, it was installed with its base about 7 m below the main floor level. Unfortunately, considerable exposure to salt water had occurred during transport of the machine from the United Kingdom and this made it necessary for a great

127

deal of work to be done to bring it into commission. Eventually, a completely new computer-controlled loading and recording system was installed. It is now possible to provide calibrations up to 550 kN with an uncertainty of about 2 in 10^5.

Besides the replacement of the control system, some mechanical modifications have been made to the machine. After evidence was received from overseas that there was a possibility of failure of some of the shackles from which the masses are suspended, these were replaced with shackles designed and manufactured in the Laboratory. The range of the machine was extended downwards by the addition of an extra stack of masses. As originally built, the machine had four stacks. The smallest force available was 10 kN. With the additional fifth stack, calibrations from 5 kN upwards are possible. This overlaps the range of 0.05 to 5.6 kN of a smaller dead-load machine in the Laboratory.

An Amsler machine capable of providing calibrations at higher values of force became available when responsibility for calibrations for the Department of Defence and the armed services was transferred from the Materials Research Laboratories, Maribyrnong, in 1978. Unlike the 550 kN machine, this does not apply gravitational loads directly but employs hydraulic amplification, nominally allowing calibrations up to 10 MN. The uncertainty is estimated to be about 3 in 10^3.

Production of Special Equipment

The importance of having provision for the production of special equipment was recognised when the Laboratory was established and instrument makers were among the early staff members. By 1944, the workshop staff totalled thirteen and there were also three draughtsmen. Many major pieces of equipment, such as interferometers and comparators, that could not be obtained from commercial suppliers, were made in the workshops. In many cases, the production of these items involved work with unusual materials and very fine tolerances.

As in other parts of the Laboratory, the workshops at the Sydney University were crowded, some being in temporary quarters separate from the main building.

The workshop building at Lindfield provided much greater space and better conditions. In 1977 a four-axis numerically controlled milling machine and a numerically controlled lathe were installed. Soon after, in 1978, a computer-aided design facility was introduced. This was the first stand-alone system of the kind to be installed in Australia and, in addition to providing for the needs of the Laboratory, it assisted many firms and organisations to assess the possibilities of similar systems for their purposes.

In recent years, the need for manufacture of special equipment has become less, partly because of the greater availability of commercially made instruments and partly because of the reduction of activities in the Laboratory requiring major special instruments. The number of tradesmen is now only about one third of the number in the early 1970s, when the demand was at its peak.

Manufacture of Optical Components

Optical components for special purposes have been produced in the Laboratory since the 1940s. While there has been some need for manufacture of lenses, much work has been concerned with optical flats and other components with flat surfaces. A major project was the production in 1960 of a Lyot-type birefringent filter transmitting a bandwidth of 0.0125 nm for use in the solar physics program. It was the largest filter of its type in the world and novel techniques were developed by Mr (later Dr) R.N. Smartt for the production of very flat surfaces on soft crystals such as calcite.

Later, the production of very flat surfaces on glass was undertaken by Mr G. Otte. He introduced a technique for polishing on Teflon-coated polishers rather than in the conventional way on pitch. This made it possible to produce flats such as those required for Fabry-Perot interferometers good to a few nanometres. Mr A.J. Leistner has developed the technique further and recently has produced flats and etalons from a range of materials including silica, Zerodur and lithium niobate. A digital interferometer system developed in the Division by Dr P. Hariharan is used to ensure that the surface accuracies are within 1 or 2 nm. The capability of the workshop to produce flats and etalons of outstanding quality has attracted attention from overseas laboratories and observatories and components for special purposes have been produced in collaborative projects.

The shop has also produced components of other shapes such as cylinders and spheres with very precise dimensional requirements. One recent project has been the polishing of a silicon sphere to be used in a determination of Avogadro's constant. This was undertaken by Leistner in collaboration with Professor G. Zosi of the Istituto di Metrologia G. Colonnetti, Turin, Italy. The sphere, made from a single crystal, has a diameter of approximately 94 mm and a mass of approximately 1 kg. With the polishing technique that was devised, it was possible to reduce deviations from roundness to less than 75 nm.

The optical workshop has assisted in the introduction of the Teflon-polishing technique into industry. It has also been able to help several Australian firms with problems in the production of various optical and other components.

References

1.   Brown, M.R., *Aust. Refrig. Air Cond. Heat.,* **29,** 18 (October 1975).

2.   Puttock, M.J., *Aust. Phys.,* **14,** 166 (1977).

The Division of Applied Physics
in 1988

After fifty years of existence, the Division of Applied Physics has many of the characteristics envisaged by those who worked for its establishment as the National Standards Laboratory. Julius, Madsen and the other members of the Secondary Industries Testing and Research Committee stated the object of the Report of the Committee was "to present a plan by which the development of secondary industry in the Commonwealth may be stimulated, and promoted on lines that have been proved essential in other countries, and by which the dependence of industry on supplies external to Australia may be minimized". They went on to point out that "the basis of any such plan must be the provision for making scientific testing and research as well as up-to-date technical knowledge readily available to industry".

In setting out its detailed proposals, the Committee called for the introduction of legislation to establish legal standards of measurement, the establishment of the National Standards Laboratory to provide the scientific basis for a uniform system of measurement, and the establishment of testing facilities. The Committee recognised that there was a need for research related to secondary industry and recommended that the Council for Scientific and Industrial Research be authorised to make proposals as to how this might be best arranged.

The CSIR Executive Committee clearly recognised the need for the staff of the Laboratory to include people trained in research and for the work on the maintenance of standards and the provision of calibration services to be associated with active research work. In the first few years after the establishment of the Laboratory, attention to the immediate problems of wartime production left little time for longer-term research. At the end of the war, the emphasis was on the development of the facilities essential for the Laboratory to function as the basic component of a national measurement system. This involved research not only to develop standards as they existed in the older standards laboratories in other counties, but also to make use of advances in physics to develop improved standards and measurement techniques.

From its beginning, the Laboratory has been involved not only in the physics of standards and measurement but also in research in other branches of physics of importance to industry and the community, particularly those in which the special facilities of the Laboratory could be used. The relative emphasis given to the various aspects of the work of the Laboratory has changed from time to time. Many contacts with industrial firms, university science departments, and government departments and instrumentalities arising from calibration work led to involvement of the Laboratory in the solution of production or scientific problems, or in collaborative investigations related to the development of new products or improved processes.

From the 1950s onwards, a considerable load has been transferred from the Laboratory to laboratories registered with the National Association of Testing Authorities. In recent years, therefore, a larger proportion of the activities of the Laboratory has been concerned with the development of its standards and measurement capability and with research not directly concerned with standards.

The research work of the Division has earned it recognition as one of the world's major national physics laboratories. Consequently, scientists from the Division are in close touch with research workers in related fields around the world and contribute with them to the extension of scientific knowledge in these fields. Although the Australian contribution is inevitably a relatively small part of the total, international recognition of the Laboratory ensures that information on new developments of significance in science and industry, wherever they occur, become available in Australia promptly.

From 1972 onwards, the work of the Division was scrutinised by eight different review committees. The most recent of these, the Review Committee on the CSIRO Division of Applied Physics (Goldsmid Committee), reporting in June 1986, noted that "The Division represents a huge resource of expertise and facilities from which the nation benefits. The management of this resource and the mechanisms for ensuring that the resource is tapped more effectively by potential users, have been the subject of numerous reviews over the last seven years. The reviews have been useful, and necessary". While they have led to some desirable changes, these reviews have been costly. They have caused serious interruptions to the scientific work of the Division, and have also involved long periods of uncertainty, with inevitable damage to morale and efficiency.

The changes to CSIRO as a whole that have been taking place in the past few years, and especially since the amended Science and Industry Research Act came into effect in December 1986 have inevitably affected the Division. As in 1938, when the Laboratory was established, there is a clear need for scientific support for Australian industry and for a sound national measurement system as a basis for industrial technology. The changes in structure and management of CSIRO are intended to stimulate interaction between CSIRO and industry, largely through collaborative projects. The Division is now expected to find a substantial part of its funds from industrial sponsors and the nature of much of its research is therefore determined by the particular interests of sponsoring firms.

With the introduction in January of a new Institute structure in CSIRO and the inclusion of the Division in the Institute of Industrial Technologies, there have been changes in its internal organisation. The activities of the Division are now organised in five programs, concerned respectively with acoustics and mechanics; electrotechnology; applied electricity and magnetism; plasmas, thin films and thermometry; and optical technology. Each program includes work related to standards and measurement as well as research and development concerned directly with industrial applications. The total number of members of the staff, which was 372 in 1980, is now 313. The proportion of the total resources of the Division devoted to standards-related activities is at approximately the same level as before the recent changes but the new arrangement is intended to allow increased flexibility in the use of resources.

The Division enters its fifty-first year with a record of achievement in research and assistance to industry and the community. The environment in which it works has changed significantly since 1938. Although it was then faced with an array of problems needing immediate attention, the philosophy of those defining the policy of CSIR was that its principal function was to undertake research in areas of significance to primary and secondary industry in Australia and to make the results of its research readily available to all who could apply them. The choice of research areas was made by the Council and the Chiefs of CSIR Divisions with the assistance of the Advisory Council and State Committees. The National Standards Laboratory was exceptional in CSIR, as a substantial part of its activities was concerned with fulfilling the statutory responsibility for providing the scientific basis of the national measurement system. It encountered problems of the same kind as other parts of CSIR, arising from the fact that, with some exceptions, there were relatively few people in secondary industry qualified to make full use of the information that it could provide.

In the intervening 50 years, there have been great changes in the structure and technological level of secondary industry and in the economic climate. In 1988, the emphasis in CSIRO is on the development of new products and manufacturing processes or the solution of problems already perceived by people in industry. The Division has already been involved in many collaborative investigations and in the 1987-88 year, external funds amounted to $1.4 million.

The November 1985 report of the Australian Science and Technology Council (ASTEC), entitled "Future directions for CSIRO", made suggestions designed to guide the Government and the CSIRO Board in deciding on the future structure, funding and operations of the Organisation. ASTEC expressed the view that "CSIRO must maintain a substantial continuing commitment to strategic basic research at a level close to that now prevailing". It considered, however, that "CSIRO should significantly increase the amount of its shorter term, more directly applicable research". ASTEC pointed out that "Most of this work will be applied research and experimental development of the sort usually conducted by industry itself in more technologically developed countries". It is against the background of these suggestions and of the decisions subsequently taken by the Board that the Division of Applied Physics will proceed to conduct its research activities and to meeting its obligations in respect of the national measurement system.